The Dominant Gene

A Novel Series about Becoming an Agile Leader

Francie Van Wirkus

The Dominant Gene is a business novel series about the journey to becoming an Agile leader. At the highest level, an Agile leader is fearless; to serve others, to learn daily, and to sense and adapt, all in the name of quality and customer value.

Each journey is different, because we are all from different industries, backgrounds, and corporate cultures. No matter your journey, you can be assured that the ride will be undulating, time consuming, and very personal. And, you will learn that the destination is not the end, but the beginning. The Dominant Gene offers an up-close view into one leader's quest to become an Agile leader: the struggles, victories, and learnings. You're invited to join main character Joel, as he leaves comfort and complacency to begin his trek of uncertainty to become an Agile leader.

It is my hope that you will be entertained, disturbed, and motivated to end your own comfy world of complacency, and begin to grow. When it gets hard, when you feel like quitting, remember you are not alone; you have me and an entire Agile community here to help.

Reveille

Book One

For Janice, a loving woman of unstoppable courage and compassion.

Thank you for sharing your wisdom, and for your relentless support and love.

Acknowledgments

Thank you to my agile-lean tribe of friends for your expertise and support. Let's celebrate this accomplishment, but not become complacent. There is still much to learn.

WATZKA LEGACY

ORGANIZATIONAL CHART

Rick - CIO

Gabriel - VP

Vladimir - VP

Ben - Director

Dipti - Director

Chase - Director

Anika - Director

THE DOMINANT GENE SERIES
REVEILLE

Lora - VP

Eve - Agile Coach

Meryll - Director

Joel - Director

Jack - Director

Cindy - Manager

Vijay - Manager

Alexis - Manager

Karen - Team Lead

Chris - Team Member

My Vision

Professional

1. To be trusted by Lora and Rick.
2. Less wasted time on conference calls.
3. Fewer ultimatum days: You can do this, but then you won't have that.

Personal

1. Eat better.
2. Support my kids' events. I miss too many of them.
3. Home by 5:30 p.m.

Hello, friends.

Welcome to the story of my agile leader journey. You can call me Joel. I thought it would be good to set some context before we dive into things. My story involves a lot of interactions that should remain private, so I'm holding back the details of my work, my company, and my family. It's not important to know them to understand my journey, because what I have learned is in my heart and mind. I've changed the names of my family members to keep their privacy, too.

I live in suburban Denver, in the beautiful state of Colorado. I'm 45, and happily married to beautiful Cele for 18 years. We met after college, at a friend's Christmas party. We have four children, whom Cele is raising instead of teaching high school math. Caroline is 15 in every sense she can be; she skis and plays basketball. But her greatest sport is hanging with friends. Elliot is 13, and into hockey and baseball. Eric is 7, and is living large. His latest interests are hockey and the violin. Then there is my adorable five year old daughter Cici, who wants to do it all.

I am an upper level technology leader in a large, complex, American corporation. Let's call the technology part of this huge company Watzka Legacy, or WL for short. I've worked there for 20 years. I'd like to say that's because I began my career when I was six, but that's not true. I began working at WL shortly after college, in my mid 20s, and grew through the ranks over the last 15 years. My title says *director*, but after the agile journey I have been on, I call myself a leader. More on that later.

Watzka Legacy has over 4,000 employees in the world headquarters alone. We sell…well, let's just say we create and sell an awesome product that requires lots of technology. In fact, technology is continually changing the game for our industry and for us. But this journey isn't about how Watzka Legacy needed to change. It's about how I needed to change.

Join me on my journey, which continues yet today. I don't have all the answers, but I have experienced explosive growth and learning these last few years. It's time I share the goodness so you, too, can become an agile leader.

Joel

Urgent

Monday January 13, 2016

RE: Agile Leader Coaching

Dear Joel,

Effective today, you have been assigned to experience agile leader coaching. We anticipate that becoming an agile organization will not be easy for anyone, and so as we begin this endeavor, I am offering my director team an agile coaching experience.

The goal is to be partially trained in agile leadership before we begin using agile in the company. The expected outcome is that you will be prepared to lead the agile transformation at Watzka Legacy.

For the next six months, you have been assigned to work with Eve, a seasoned agile coach. She will contact you shortly with all of the details.

I look forward to hearing about how things are going when I return from India.

Regards,

Lora

Three Amigos

"This is so *Lora* to pull a stunt like this," Meryll huffed as she paced the floor of my office, clenching Lora's memo.

She had a point, but I was so used to Lora dumping on us, the memo approach didn't bother me. We were her direct reports, so we got dumped on in person, in our absence, and in memos like the one we had just received.

"The real stunt will be getting coaching," Jack sighed and sat down in one of my guest chairs.

I raised my Starbucks cup. "Yep."

Meryll was still pacing. My office is nice, but it's not big enough for two of us to be sitting, and a third to be pacing back and forth like a caged hyena. These days, most rooms are too small for Meryll. Not because she's big, well, she's gained weight over the years, but not that much. Lately she's been very intense, and I'm not sure why. I'm sure as hell not going to ask her right now.

"She doesn't say that *she's* getting any coaching. How's that going to work?" Meryll paused and took in the view out my office window.

"The way it always does, Meryll. You know the drill." Jack smirked. "So why don't you sit down and drink your flat chai latte with extra marshmallow topping before it gets cold."

"There is no marshmallow topping, moron." Meryll grabbed her cup and sat down in my other guest chair.

I had to reach out, before she wound herself too tight. "Flat white at Christmas time, but now back to the more austere coconut milk single shot latte, right?"

Her perfectly done face softened. "Correct. It's what civilized people drink."

Jack rolled his eyes. "Well, now that we have Meryll's foo-foo drink of choice identified, what are we going to do about this coaching?"

"It's probably just another Lora fad. Let's ride it out until the next urgent message comes out," I said. "It can't be that hard; it's just going to be a huge time sucker."

"I didn't know people even wrote memos anymore," Jack said with a confused look.

God bless Jack, the new guy. He's been with the company for six months, and he still thinks Watzka Legacy (from herein I will call WL) is so much more modern than it really is.

Meryll sat back in her chair. We've been working together the last five years, so I know some of her reactions to Lora's ideas. This is usually the part when she makes a decision.

"Well, I certainly don't have time for coaching. Good luck getting on my calendar." Decision made.

"I've lived through more annoying things from Lora than this," I shrugged.

Jack's smirk remained. It's one of the things I like about him: he wants to have fun, even when he is not having fun.

"Yes, probably just an annoyance." He looked at his smart phone. "I gotta roll. Gotta bunch of one-on-ones today."

Meryll checked her Tiffany watch. "Ooo, me too. Talk again next week?"

"Unless we get coached out of our jobs." Jack winked at us as he opened my office door.

First Impressions

"We are contracted to meet for six months, but I offer all of my clients a 30-day trial. If we just can't seem to get along, it's no use pushing through." Eve smiled at me. She looked 40-ish, very fit, and very polished. Pretty, but not overdone. Not very corporate looking. Large diamond wedding ring, but minimal jewelry. She doesn't scream out democrat, but that's probably the case. She might have cats.

"Like a Two Feet Rule, Joel."

"What?"

"Although it's a huge commitment, you are not a prisoner in this coaching experience. In the first 30 days, you have two feet to walk away whenever you wish." Eve's green eyes were steady. "No harm, no foul."

"Sounds fair." I shifted in my chair.

"You have doubts."

"I—my director, Lora shoved this at me drive-by style. It doesn't feel like the Two Feet Rule will hold up to her mandate." How much should I tell her? How much does she know? What the hell is going on, anyway?

"Thank you for being honest with me, Joel. We do need to talk about that." Eve went back to her coaching contract. "Let's get through the rest of this agreement first."

Eve led us through what looked like a very straightforward coaching agreement. Not that I know anything about coaching agreements. Nothing was too startling. Then again, I work for Lora. Years of her management has probably rendered me desensitized to what's outrageous.

Basically, I have to commit to make time to meet with her twice a week, offer her access to my surrounding teams to gather ongoing feedback, and be open and honest. Maybe this isn't going to blow over.

"The Breakthrough Coaching model is different, Joel, not in when we meet or how often, but in the challenges. And, it's only as effective as you are honest."

"Let me get this straight, Eve. My director is forcing me to go through coaching, and I'm supposed to be as open and honest as I can be?" And, with a woman?! I'm around enough bossy women all day long. I'm not a chauvinist, but spilling my most honest thoughts to Eve…well, maybe I am a chauvinist.

Eve smiled. Clearly she's heard my objection before. "I'm not in your situation, but I understand it. Unfortunately, yes, you are being shoved into this." She paused.

The silence killed me. "This is the part where you tell me there is always a choice, and that working for Lora is my choice, and that working for WL is also my choice."

"Only if I was some creepy old-school HR director." Eve opened her hands on the table. "I would like to just get through these ground rules, and then we can get to know each other, and talk about whatever is on your mind or in your heart."

"I'm sorry. I should stop interrupting you with my jadedness."

"Apology accepted." Eve grinned. So she has a soul. This is good.

I kept my mouth shut, and we got through the rest of Eve's coaching spiel. I thought it very curious that she never mentioned the word "agile" once, and yet, Lora directed this as an agile coaching experience. I held my questions for later.

"Where would you like to meet?" Eve asked. She was definitely an athlete of some kind.

I shrugged. "To save time, would you like to meet at my office?"

"I'd like to meet outside the walls of Watzka Legacy. It's easier to relax, and to see things from afar. How about J&L's Café?"

This was weird. We've always been encouraged to use our internal café. I hesitated for a moment. Lora would never support this. I'm going to meet with a coach for 2-4 hours a week…away from the office? What if there is an emergency?

"Lora knows you'll be meeting me offsite regularly."

Well, then… "J&L's has great coffee. I'm up for that."

"I love their matcha lattes. Just enough boost." Eve grinned. "We'll go Dutch. No pressure."

"Is that where you take all of your victims?"

"Only the difficult cases."

"All righty, then."

"Great. We are set to begin tomorrow. I need notice of any change in the schedule at least 24 hours ahead of our meeting time. Life is not perfect, so I'll give you one mulligan, one missed appointment. Any other missed appointments, and our relationship is in jeopardy."

"Roger that."

"Everything we discuss is confidential, unless you are going to break a law. Then I am obligated to share with law enforcement. I will tell you if I do this."

"Coaching is confidential, even from Lora? You're not going to have one-on-ones with her to let her know how I'm progressing?"

"Confidential. No one else will know the content of our sessions. I will not be meeting with Lora. She is aware of how this coaching model works." Eve was intent. "Enough on the rules." She packed her signed contracts, and focused on me. "I want us to get to know each other a bit before we dive into the process. Ask me anything you like."

"I'm sort of full up right now, Eve. I'm not sure I want to know more."

"Not one question comes to mind…" she trailed off. It was more of a challenge than a question.

"How long have you been coaching?"

"Ten years." Her green eyes sparkled. "I started when I was 15."

"Nice. Me too. I mean, managing people." Time to move past formalities, or we'll probably end up talking about her cats. "Did Lora send us all to coaching because we are bad directors?"

Eve is pleased with this question. "Joel, your coaching assignment is not a punishment."

"Well, at WL, that's usually the case. You screw up, you get put on an action plan, and you get coaching. Well, I don't know anyone who got coaching from an outside company, but…"

"We're going to do Breakthrough Coaching for agile." Eve announced. "It's not a punishment, a sentence, or anything negative. In fact, it should be an exponentially positive force in your life." Eve leaned forward. "You are good, Joel. But you need to get better. Lora recognizes this in her team. I find that encouraging."

So much for holding that against Lora. I'm getting coaching because she believes in me. At least, on a superficial level.

"Is Lora getting coached?"

"Not by me. Not by my firm."

"That means no?"

"She told me she was looking for an agile coach. I gave her my recommendations, and that was the end of it."

Classic Lora, as Meryll would say. We all need fixing, but she doesn't. She'll say she's looking for a coach, maybe even say that she uses one, but she won't. She's not going to make herself that vulnerable, even for this huge transformation that's on the horizon.

No use worrying about *her*. I'm going to have an exponentially positive experience. I can hardly stand the anticipation.

"Any other questions, Joel?"

"How many cats do you have?"

Eve laughs. "I don't have any cats. No pets."

"Huh." Maybe she's not so bad after all.

Session 1

As I walk to J&L's Café, I fight the negative feelings of having a coach. There must be some ulterior motive. With the agile transformation looming, someone's probably got an agenda. And with Jack, Meryll, and I as directors in the thick of things, we will have targets on our backs. Drive and deliver, or get out. I've seen it before. Just because it's an agile transformation doesn't mean it's going to be any different. Why should I take a complete stranger's word for it that this assignment is positive?

If I'm caught up in this, so are Meryll and Jack. When will they be pushed into having their first session? For all I know, they could be meeting their coaches at J&L's at the same time. *Meh*, probably not. This coaching operation feels very intentional. I stalked Eve on social media, and she seems legit. Tons of agile and lean experience. Lots of recommendations and favorable words about her work. Many from people who were part of an agile transformation. She's married with kids and appears to be normal. As if I know what normal looks like working at WL. I researched Breakthrough Coaching. It's also legit. But it's not agile coaching.

After getting my usual house blend I meet Eve, where she is savoring her matcha latte. She's got a mini laptop open, as well as a new notebook and pen. She could pull off a stock photo for a company brochure. Except she looks a little too…something. It doesn't matter, and so I find myself sitting across from her.

Eve smiled. "Right on time, Joel. Thank you."

"Whew. I passed the first test."

"Are you ready?"

"Sure."

She studies my face. "You don't look ready. I don't pretend to know you, but you don't look ready."

"Is this really confidential?"

"Yes, Joel. Everything we discuss is confidential unless--"

"I know, unless I'm gonna break the law."

Eve opened her mini laptop. "You got it."

"I'm also struggling with how I will have time for this. I've got a packed schedule."

"We'll make it happen." Eve was missing the point.

"Right. At what cost? Or, am I supposed to just cram this in on top of everything else I have responsibility for?" I realized I'm getting a little contentious. "I'm sorry, Eve. I shouldn't push on you like this. It's just…because of the way this 'coaching experience' was handed down via email, I haven't had a chance to share what I think about it with Lora."

"Thank you, and no harm done. Given the way this went down, I'm actually surprised you are here this morning. I am very happy you came."

"Sure. But do you know what I'm asking?"

"Yes. Is this like night school, or is it accepted as part of your day?"

"Right."

"Here's my understanding of our relationship: you have been given permission and time by Lora and Rick to meet with me offsite. And we can do it as often as we need to in a given week."

"This is so jacked up, and it's not even begun yet. You don't get a fair chance because I'm pissed about things, and I don't get a fair chance because I'm pissed about things."

Eve smiled. "It's okay that you are pissed. You are always entitled to your own feelings."

"Were you a counselor before this gig?"

Eve laughed. "No, actually, I worked for a software company."

I wanted to know more about it, but this wasn't the time to go there. Like I said to Eve, I was pissed, not curious. Today is shaping up to be a challenge. What's new?!

"I want us to get to the part of our meeting where we focus on you, instead of how the universe will push against you to work with me. Please trust me that we'll circle back to the part about how to find time for coaching. In the meantime, it's very important that you attend every session we agree to."

"Got it." No doubt about it, this is going to be night school. *Just another thing.*

"You are probably agreeing with me because you feel required to do so. I hope someday soon, you agree to commit to our time together because you *want* to. I want to prove my value and the value of this coaching process to you."

"I don't understand why I need a coach. I'm a seasoned director, with tons of experience driving for results, and getting them. Time and again, my teams deliver and meet their goals. We are not perfect, but we are successful. The same goes for Jack and Meryll. Well, Jack is the new guy, but he hasn't messed up yet."

Eve kept her professional smile. "I can give you an answer today, Joel. Yet I believe you will find a new answer after we work together."

"So…why?"

"Studies have proven that people reach their highest potential through coaching. Not through wishing they could be better, or by reading industry books. And certainly not by being forced to by their VP."

I chuckle. "So, this is going to be good for me, no matter my current circumstances?"

"Yes. Why not trust me? Forget your current circumstances, and just do it because you want to reach your highest potential. Here at WL, or anywhere. See where it takes you." She leans forward. "Well, where *you* take it."

I really have no objection now. She's officially neutralized all of my hang ups. "I can't resist a challenge, even from a complete stranger who has been assigned to me." I sigh, but I'm smiling. "I am ready, Eve."

"Excellent."

Eve fishes in her bag, and pulls out a small, leather-bound notebook. She slides it across the table, and tells me it's a gift from her to me. I open it. My name is on the inside, along with lots of blank, lined pages. Great, she wants me to keep a diary. That means I'm probably going to have to talk about my childhood.

"Don't be a hater before you know what it's for, Joel." Eve tilts her head and tries to meet my eyes. I'm averting them to the ceiling like my teenage daughter Caroline would do.

She waits. I stall. Finally, I come around and look at her again, but say nothing. Eve smirks, thoroughly enjoying my teenager moment.

"It's a notebook for you to document your reflections and learnings from our sessions together."

"Dear diary…" I snark, clasping my hands under my chin.

"Only if you want to." Eve sighs. "Your agile leader journey is going to be long, convoluted, foggy, and occasionally, pretty awesome. Also, we are going to focus a lot on reflection. Using this notebook can help you keep track of it. There is something about writing things in a notebook that makes them special. More special than notes on a tablet or a laptop. I believe when something is special, it is memorable. Capturing these memorable moments helps you grow, and measure your growth. And I won't be reviewing it at any time. I want you to use it, but it's purely a private exercise in tracking your growth."

"Fair enough." I examine it closer. "This is a really nice notebook. Thank you Eve."

"Enjoy the ride Joel."

Eve tells me how she's going to ask me what I want, both professionally and personally. I know she said it was all confidential, but it's still very uncomfortable to trust her. She shows me the template she is using to capture all of my professional and personal wants. She tells me she will share it with me after each session. She also tells me this list is what we'll use to build my vision (I'm going to have a vision?!). Fair enough.

Eve checks her watch. Looks like one of those Timex Ironman styles. "So Joel, at 8:00 a.m. on January 26, 2016, what do you want?"

I am stuck already. I shake my head in chagrin. "This is weird."

"It is," Eve encouraged. "Today, how many people are going to take time like this and ask you what you truly want out of life? It should feel good that I care."

"Maybe that's the weird part."

"That it feels good?"

"That you care."

"Huh." She has not typed a word yet. "Would you like people to care about what you want?"

"Yes, that would be nice."

"This sounds important. Which people need to care? Who specifically?"

"Lora. And our CIO, Rick. Don't get me wrong here, I feel very cared for by my family, and I love them for it. But Lora and Rick…they are different."

"What about your immediate peers, Meryll and Jack?"

"They care. But they are *positioned* not to care. Does that make sense?"

"Sounds environmental."

"Yes. Probably because of Lora and Rick."

"Fair enough, but we'll hold off on a diagnosis for a while longer. Let's go on to what else you want Joel."

For the moment, I let go of the pain around Lora, and focus again on me. "I want…to know where I stand with Lora, more than during a one-on-one meeting. There is not enough transparency."

"Got it. Transparency." Eve looks like she's heard this problem before.

My nerves cause me to suck down my coffee too fast. Good thing I have a bottle of water with me.

"What else do you want?" Peppercorn ranch, house vinaigrette, Caesar…

Another pause while I sort through honest wants from regular gripes.

"I want to spend less time on conference calls that I don't own, that don't seem to add value." I sigh. Huge swaths of time are spent with me making forced appearances.

"Got it. What about in-person meetings? Do you have any of those that seem wasteful, and yet required?"

I laugh. "Of course. Aren't those just an accepted fact of being a tech director in corporate America?"

"You tell me. Do you want to change it, whether it is or is not an accepted fact in corporate America?" Green eyes patiently wait for me.

"Yes, I want to change it. I want to spend my time in a more valuable way."

We went on like this for 45 minutes. When we finished, I had quite a list of professional and personal wants. These are things I want, and they are also things that are exciting to me. When I think about them and talk about them, I have positive energy and feel good. Who doesn't want to work on a list like that? Sure, some of these things are huge and difficult to achieve. But I think that's where Eve comes in. Eve emailed me my list:

Professional wants

I want...

Lora to care about me and the team.

Rick to care about me and the team.

To work in an environment where people care about each other.

To know where I stand with Lora. Transparency.

Less wasted time on conference calls.

Less wasted time during in-person meetings.

Less time creating reports that seem to be a duplicate of other reports.

Less wasted time dealing with Lora's dysfunction.

Believe that what I do matters.

Believe that what my teams do matters.

Fewer ultimatum days: you can do this, but then you won't have that.

To be trusted by Lora and Rick.

A better view into what my teams are doing.

A better view into what my teams have accomplished.

My teams are thought leaders of the company. They are, but no one knows it.

Our area publishes simpler metrics.

To have a better way to support my teams' work.

Professional Wants, continued

To grow my teams, both managers and staff.

To delegate more to my assistant, Marilyn.

To delegate more to my managers.

Less blaming by my teams.

Less taking the blame of other teams.

Better accountability by my managers and their teams.

No work on Saturdays or Sundays.

Personal Wants

More time with my family.

Home by 5:30 p.m.

Better quality workouts. I just rush through them now.

Eat better.

Ironman Boulder 2017!

Take Cele and the kids on that bike vacation in Spain. We keep postponing it.

Support my kids' events. I miss too many of them.

More time with my friends.

"This list is from this moment in time. It might change by the next time we meet, and that's okay. Speaking of next time, we're on for this Thursday at 8:00 a.m."

I check my phone. There is a weekly conference call with Lora's offshore connections in India at the same time. It's a can't-miss episode, although usually nothing new arises.

"I can't do eight. I can do 9:30 a.m." I scroll through the day. "No, wait, 9:30 won't work. How about…" There is no time on Thursday. I put my phone down in defeat and look blankly at Eve.

"You are full up on Thursday?"

"Yes. Sorry."

"Can't move anything?"

"No, I—I don't think so. How about Friday at 8:00 a.m.?"

Eve checks her calendar. "Sure."

"Thanks."

"On Friday we'll review what it is you want, both professionally and personally. Then, we'll prioritize the list, and begin to build your vision."

"Sounds good." I'm already thinking about the user experience steering meeting I have to attend in 24 minutes.

"We talked about a lot of things, Joel. Thank you for your honesty. And, for giving this a chance."

"You're welcome."

"Anything you want to discuss before Friday, just give me a call. I'm here to help."

I left our meeting feeling exhausted. It was weird, because nothing else happened but me telling Eve what I wanted. She just kept asking, and to my surprise, I just kept telling her things. A simple formula that seemed to work really well. Her easy, professional style made a difference too. I like her, even though I don't want to like her.

Watzka must be paying a fortune to have me, Meryll and Jack coached. At one point in the process, Eve had asked me, "What would make 2016 a great year?" I mentioned a few work and family things that are on the list above. Curiously, none of my answers to this question were things that are currently on my performance goals. Ouch! I'm in worse shape than I imagined.

As much as I thought things were going along pretty well, many things bothered me. Things that happened every day, every month, every year, and yet I did nothing to change them. Most of them were just swept under the rug. At the end of the day, here's what I wrote in my notebook:

Reflections

I am being forced into coaching that I don't need.

Coaching is night school. Lots of conflicts, and pressure to fit it all in.

What I want and my goals for the year are not the same.

My job annoys me, and I have been suppressing it.

Where is agile in this agile coaching?

I like my notebook.

Night School

The next day, my email was exploding with messages from Lora. Ugly ones, with long, precarious strings of conversation that had occurred in the last week. Some were forwarded to me, some were directly sucking me in. I was struggling to plow through one problem, when my assistant Marilyn walked in. She works for me, Lora, Meryll and Jack. She's fantastic.

"Sorry to interrupt, but Lora wants to crash your Friday morning conference call, and there are two more meetings cropping up here as a result of that."

"She's in India. Isn't that like a 15-hour time difference?"

"Actually, 12.5 hours. That means she's got time in the evening that translates to 8:00 a.m. Friday morning."

"Great. Right over my coaching."

"You have an opening at 11:00 a.m., so I called Eve and she was able to reschedule her things to accommodate you."

"Thank you," I sigh. "Marilyn, you helped me dodge another bullet. I appreciate it."

"No problem."

Friday morning's conference call yielded another meeting for me and my manager team. Of course it was scheduled for 11:00 a.m., so of course Marilyn had to contact Eve. Unfortunately, Eve had no other availability Friday, and refused to meet me on a Saturday or Sunday. I was irritated, but didn't I say I wanted to stop working on the weekends? After a good 15 minutes of calendar searching, we pull the plug. We had to skip our second meeting, and just plan on getting together at 8:00 a.m. on Tuesday.

With another matcha latte and medium house blend on the table, Eve gave me an earful. I heard about how important our time together is, and that I need to stick to my commitments. She did it in a way that didn't make me feel like I was five, which was refreshing.

"You don't know Lora. This type of disruption happens 52 weeks of the year."

"Are you saying this coaching experience with me is no match for Lora?"

"Basically, yes. Everything Lora is involved in becomes a train wreck."

"Train wreck?"

"Emotional train wreck, calendar train wreck, team train wreck…take your pick."

Eve is thoughtful. I would be too if I were coaching this mess. "She made it clear that this agile coaching experience was critical for her direct reports."

"I'm sure she did. And, at the same moment, she is expecting me to clone myself, and appear in two places at once. Lora is very talented at having a vision of one thing, and then leading it out in a different direction. And then, oops, she forgets to share that she's moved in a different direction." I tried not to gulp my house blend. It was especially comforting that morning. Eve waited for more. "No way to win with her."

"All right. I see where you stand. And, I appreciate your honesty. Let's try to move past this example, so we don't spend our entire time talking about this. Well, we're going to end up talking about Lora, just not this meeting fiasco."

Easy for her to say. I'm beginning to feel like this coaching will have a black or white outcome. Either nothing will change and it will be an exercise in futility, or I will make progress (whatever that is) and win Lora's favor. I realize Lora's not under my control, but if things work out, I'll be on her good side. No matter that *she* won't get coaching or make any changes.

Speaking of things out of my control, Eve informed me that part of my agile coaching experience was going to include getting feedback from my direct reports and their teams. She wanted to get a baseline measure, here at the beginning, and then a few times along the way. She told me exactly how she would do it: visiting teams and managers together at their weekly meeting, and then explain that she needed their candid feedback about me. She planned to give them a sheet with five questions on it:

1. Describe the strengths of your director Joel.
2. Describe the weaknesses of your director Joel.
3. What advice do you have for Joel?
4. What would you change about the leadership team above Joel?
5. What is the number one obstacle to your team's productivity?

Teams and managers would have 30-45 minutes to complete the questions, talk about them as a group, and submit compiled feedback to Eve. She was concerned that I wouldn't be up to the challenge of making myself so vulnerable to the team. I was more in shock that she was going to request taking over an entire team meeting on my behalf. Talk about their director for an hour? In fact, she was on the team's agenda for *this week*. Imagine!

I accepted the challenge. I wasn't thrilled about it, but I wasn't going to cower away either. Why fight this experience now? I planned to fold into it, and see where I landed. That is still the plan. Besides, so far it was as entertaining as it was fascinating.

"Joel, today we're going to review your professional and personal wants, and then prioritize them. If you have thought of something that needs to be added to the list, or taken off, just speak up. Otherwise, we'll push forward with what you have."

Sounded simple enough. Yet going through that list again was tough. Even after grouping similar wants together, everything on it seemed important. And, it seemed to stir up even more problems.

I want...

Professional wants

1. To be trusted by Lora and Rick.
2. Less wasted time on conference calls.
3. Fewer ultimatum days: You can do this, but then you won't have that.

Personal Wants

1. Eat better.
2. Support my kids' events. I miss too many of them.
3. Home by 5:30 p.m.

"Joel, these six things are very powerful. In fact, they are what will comprise your vision for our work."

"They are very powerful things. If we accomplish them, life will be grand. But…is this agile coaching?"

"It *is* agile coaching. Trust me." Next thing you know, she'll be catching flies with chopsticks.

"I do trust you." I laugh to myself. "You're going to my teams this week to ask them what they think of me."

Eve took a breath. "I am so very grateful that you have given me your trust. That means a lot. Especially in light of the way you were pushed into it."

"If you send me away today with an assignment to paint a fence, I may give up on you," I chided.

Eve rolled her eyes. "If only I could be as good at coaching as Mr. Miyagi."

"If you can get Lora and Rick to trust me, you win."

"All right, back to work here. Let's take a look at the core issues of what holds Lora and Rick back from trusting you."

"Man, I need another cup."

"Go ahead." Eve said. "I'll wait right here." It's as if she knew what was coming, without really knowing what was coming. She really is a professional. And, she really cares how difficult this is for me.

"I'm joking."

"So let's look at that number one professional want of yours, to be trusted by Lora and Rick."

"We might be here all day."

"Feel good about that. In our coaching sessions we can talk about 100 things in our time, or just one. If it takes us three weeks to work through it, that's what we'll do. It's your vision, your pace."

"All righty then."

"So, on trust…do you know for a fact that Lora and Rick don't trust you? Have they told you?"

"It's not that simple. I haven't ever heard Lora or Rick say it. It's more in their actions."

"Can you give me an example?"

"Sure." There are so many examples. How to give her one that really crystalizes my point…

"You're searching for a perfect one. Doesn't need to be perfect."

I give Eve a Lora example. Just a few months ago, our team was considering visiting some companies already using agile and lean. Lora told us to find the companies we were interested in, and book time for all of us to visit. Meryll and I did just that, but when we shared the information with Lora, she took it, and then visited them with Rick instead of with us.

When we challenged her about being left out of the loop, Lora first pretended to not understand. We reminded her that the original reason for visiting these companies came from a discussion with the four of us. Lora said she didn't remember that being the case. Then Meryll was labeled as "emotional" and

Jack and I were "whiners," and insecure about our jobs. The meeting ended on a sour note, leaving Jack, Meryll and me in the dust.

To make matters worse, Lora made a huge deal about all the things she and Rick learned while visiting these companies. Presentations were spun up, and Lora basked in the attention. Rick appeared to go along with it. He probably knew nothing about the switch.

"Thank you for sharing, Joel." She's not fake. But she's almost too nice.

"Do you have to thank me every time I tell you a story?"

"You're uncomfortable?"

"Yeah. It seems overdone."

"I want to be very clear how much I appreciate your honesty."

I keep smiling, but say nothing.

"How about I try to dial it back to thanking you once, at the end of our time together?"

"Sure."

"Okay. How about Rick? It didn't seem like he was implicated in the debacle you just described. Can you give me an example of Rick not trusting you?"

"That's easy. He has bi-monthly one-on-ones with all of us, and with Lora."

"Really. Twice a month?"

"Yeah." I chuckle. "In the meetings, he asks the same questions of me, Jack and Meryll. Often, he'll ask us about each other's work. The worst part is how he gets down into the weeds of what we're doing. It's really interesting how many notes he takes to keep all the details straight."

"Wow."

"I'm not sure I told you this, but the three of us meet in my office once a week, just to cope with everything."

"No, but that sounds like a good idea. The three amigos."

"Ahead of these one-on-ones, we use our time together to make sure we share what each of us is going to say to Rick."

"That sounds like waste." Eve swirls her drink.

"Sure it is. But it's the way to get by."

"Does he ask you about Lora's work?"

"Yes. I usually just gloss over it so I don't have to actually talk to him about how bad she can be." The words that just came out…shocked me. I can't speak for a moment.

Eve smirked. "And you thought everything was fine."

"Maybe not as fine as originally thought. Your trust questions have stirred up some stories that I've forgotten about." I sip water. "Even right now, Lora is in India working with our clients. The trip was booked a long time ago, but wasn't on her calendar until last week. Jack saw the entry 'hold for vacation' a while ago. He asked her about it, just for conversation's sake. Lora mentioned visiting her aunt in Miami, and that was the end of it."

"Meryll's a strong player with the India business?"

"Yes. With the relationships Meryll has with them, she should be there with Lora, or even with her own managers. Our partners in India love her, and she's never done anything bad with the accounts." I sigh. "It probably has nothing to do with Meryll. It's all about Lora, and what's in her head."

Eve said it was a good place to stop. But she wasn't finished with me. I got my first agile coaching assignment. It didn't seem very agile at all.

"Thank you, Joel," Eve grins, "for your honesty today."

"You're welcome." I'm still not comfortable, but I appreciate her effort.

"We are just getting rolling on your vision, but I'd like to start work on making a change. I hate to be all talk and no substance." She types on her mini laptop. "Can you think of one, small thing you can do to begin moving the needle on getting Lora and Rick to trust you more?"

There is a long pause. There are probably crickets, too, but it's too noisy in the café to hear them.

"One small thing…" Eve encouraged.

"Nothing is small with those two." I have to come up with something before she does. "I see what you're trying to do, but this distrust thing is a lot bigger than just me, Jack and Meryll."

"Keep thinking."

"Lora loves reports. I could make a new one for her."

"Nope. Not very agile, Joel."

"Ah, but you're not being fair. You wanted me to move the needle on her trust. You didn't request that it be very agile."

"Making a report for the sake of a report, in the end, will not build trust."

"Can I think about it, and we can talk about it next time?" I'm reaching. "Lora's not back from India for two more days."

"I need you to commit to taking a step toward building trust with Lora." She's a persistent bugger.

"Fine, fine. How about this: I'll get on her calendar for when she's back from India. I can meet her for a coffee walk. You know, as a way to ask her about her trip to India. I never do that with her."

"Excellent, Joel!" Eve lit up.

"Whew. I'm off the hook."

"I'll add that to your plan, here. Oh, and you have 24 hours to call me if you have any change of heart or reservations about this breakthrough. Otherwise, you're locked and loaded. Also, don't forget, the next time we get together, we'll be reviewing feedback from your teams."

I left our meeting worn out, and it was only 10:30 a.m. We covered a lot of stuff, and much of it were things that I had repressed, just to keep progressing. I forget how much I don't like the way Lora treats me, Jack and

Francie Van Wirkus

Meryll. I forget how Rick is a micromanager who can't let go of anything. I've just learned to deal with them, and find my way. It was a good idea at the time. After talking with Eve, it's beginning to feel like maybe that approach is flawed.

Reflections

Our team lacks trust.

Rick and Lora do not trust us.

I am going to do my part to build trust with Lora and Rick.

I deal with a lot of emotional crap, daily.

Where is agile in this agile coaching?

Stronger Together

"I researched all of them on social media. They are legit." Jack confirmed.

"Of course they are." Meryll stopped pacing, and sat down. "I wonder why I got the girl and you got the boy, but Joel got a girl?"

"You sound like you're in sixth grade," Jack said.

"You know what she's making me do?" Meryll asks. "Get feedback from my teams about me. She's actually going to their team meetings."

"Same here," I say.

"Huh." Jack is impressed, and scared. "I guess that means I'm next."

"Count on it." I assure him.

"I'm having serious FOMO right now," Jack sighs. "I haven't even met with my coach yet."

Meryll giggles. She's moved on from us. "If Lora goes through coaching, she'll never agree to such…vulnerability."

"No." Jack shook his head. "She will never, ever do something like this. *We* need fixing, not her."

Reflections

Jack, Meryll and I need each other on this journey.

Francie Van Wirkus

Feedback from Hell

Ahead of our next meeting, Eve sent me the feedback from my teams. She wanted me to have a chance to read through it, and reflect on it. That move never happens at WL. You never give the feedback "ahead of time." Such courtesies only cause problems in our culture.

She was fast, too. I had no idea how she was able to meet with all three of my teams and compile the feedback. She is some sort of feedback ninja.

The bottom line: this is the worst feedback I've ever received. Wow.

1. **Describe the strengths of your director Joel.**
   Nice dresser.
   He keeps us from Lora.
   He sends us to conferences.
   He values learning.
   If we want to go to a class or get a book, we can.
   He has good ideas.
   Strategic thinker.
   Not afraid of anything.

2. **Describe the weaknesses of your director Joel.**
   Doesn't listen during meetings.
   Interrupts during meetings.
   Doesn't respect our time-pulls us aside any old time to talk about what's on his mind.
   Doesn't respect our time-goes long.
   Doesn't respect our knowledge, experiences.
   Does whatever Lora tells him.
   Arrives late to meetings.
   After arriving late for a meeting, jumps in right of way, often making us double back.
   Doesn't consider intent before talking.

Describe the weaknesses of your director Joel, continued.

Defensive.
Access—hard to find him.
Access—hard to know if he is avoiding us or just buried.

3. **What advice do you have for Joel?**
Think about your intent before attending a meeting.
Think about how talented and smart your teams are, and how you don't use them.
What are you defending?
Stop using our one-on-one sessions for your purposes.
Stop pushing your agenda in "I want to offer you some background..."

4. **What would you change about the leadership team above Joel?**
Get new ones!
More transparency—tell us what is going on.
Trust us.
Trust us: seems like we have to make a ton of reports that all say the same thing.
Share more of your vision.
Meet us for coffee or lunch.
We have tried to have lunch with them and we're told they don't have lunch with people at our level.

5. **What is the number one obstacle to your team's productivity?**
Our leadership team.
Dependencies.
Silos: we don't know what other teams are doing.

Francie Van Wirkus

Pretty much the feedback from hell. Thank God Lora doesn't get to see this. At least, I have to trust Eve that Lora won't see it. Yes, I am a strategic, learning-loving roadblock. I interrupt people too. I'm awful.

I can't believe this is what teams think of me. Don't they know the difference between driving for results and dictator? No. They don't see it from my perspective because they don't *have* my perspective. And, for some reason, offering my perspective is a criminal offense.

I'm not a victim, here, but it takes a certain drive and determination to lead our area. The goals we are given are huge, and the bar is set really high. I can't afford to have it blown to pieces by people who don't have the right perspective. And, they don't know what it's like to put up with Lora and Rick. In fact, half of my managers probably wouldn't survive working for Lora and Rick.

All of that relationship building takes time, pretty much all of my time. So I don't have any time to spend with teams. Besides, isn't that why I have managers? I hired them because they were good people, with good hearts, and the ability to navigate the HR spaghetti at Watzka.

Then I think about how much blame happens within my teams, and between my teams and other departments. It's nonstop. Of course they are going to blame me and those above me, if given the chance. There are only a handful of people who are accountable and have the perspective to see the entire system. I'd like to think I'm one of them. We're needed everywhere, and so we're constantly booked in meetings. It might not match my job description, but it's what's needed from me right now.

That's also why I'm late to many meetings. There's too much to keep the pace. There are too many people to please in a day. And if I arrive late, am I supposed to just say nothing? What's the point of going then? These are some messed up teams. Agile is going to be really good for them.

Beyond how uncomfortable it was to take in all of this feedback, it was strange. It didn't match my experience at Watzka. It wasn't my current reality. I wanted to blame Eve for some reason. Maybe she didn't deliver the assignment right.

"Asking for this feedback was a brave move, Joel."

Who was she kidding? "You made me do it."

"You didn't have to do it." Eve encouraged.

"I didn't know I had a choice."

Eve sighed. She had to know this was difficult to digest. "Okay, so you were a little pushed." Eve reminded me of how she wants to have a full view of my world. Yes, of course, the more she knows the better she can help me. I understand this is the process. I don't have to like it.

"Before we dig into it, can you tell me how your breakthrough assignment went? You were going to do one thing to move the needle on establishing better trust between you and Lora. Did you take that coffee walk with Lora, or at least schedule it?"

"I have time scheduled with her tomorrow. I booked it separately, just like you asked, not baked into an existing one-on-one meeting."

Eve was pleased. "Tomorrow is good. We will circle back on how it went at our next meeting. Now, are you ready to dig into the feedback?"

"I'm pretty new to this coaching thing. I had no idea what I was getting into." I sip my house blend. "This is too much. And, it doesn't have anything to do with agile."

"Yes, there is a ton of feedback, here. Please know that our coaching takes into account that you can't be all things to all people. There will always be unhappy people. Yet this feedback is a summary of the majority of your teams. They are not one-off statements. It's real, and we need to use it."

I sigh.

Eve can feel my defeat. I like that. "I don't think there is anything you could have done to better prepare yourself for facing it. Just let it be what it is."

"Crappy."

"Ok. But not all of it."

I open my hands. "So now what?"

"Joel, I know you may not believe it, but this feedback is a gift for you."

God, I have used that on my managers. My stomach turned into a knot.

"You look pale."

I tell Eve how I use that line on my managers, but it's never been used on me. Eve says it's not a "line," that feedback truly is a gift. That fact has been lost on me here at WL. So we get into how I can best use this gift to make me better.

"Joel, most leaders do not mean harm to their teams. Their intentions are usually good, but they are lost in the pressures, the culture, and the ego."

"You haven't worked with Lora or her ego."

"You're right. But do you hear what I'm saying? This feedback is exactly what you need to begin your agile leader journey. None of us are perfect, so as leaders, you're not going to get all good feedback."

"What does any of this have to do with agile?"

Eve sits back, then leans forward. I think she's trying to break through to my thick head. "You're training for your first Ironman triathlon in 2017, right?"

"Yes. Ironman Boulder." I'm chilled. The thought of doing Ironman Boulder in my current out of shape state is nearly as frightening as this feedback.

"Okay. You can't just go out and swim 2.4 miles, or ride 112 miles, or run a marathon. The risk of failure is huge. Well, you could make the distance, but it would be a horrible experience, and take a very long time. Before doing such an epic challenge, you need to train your body first, right?"

"Yes."

"Strengthen your core, maybe some weight training for your shoulders to be strong enough to swim and to sit on that bike in aero position for over five hours...agile is an Ironman, Joel. You can just go out and do it, but it will take you forever, be very painful, and you are at great risk not to succeed. Think of our initial coaching as your core training. We are building you up, getting you strong, so you can better absorb agile."

"Huh." She sure knows a lot about Ironman. She's probably done a bunch of them when she's not pounding leaders like me.

"Now we are at the pain point: You believed your leadership style, motives and values were good enough for agile." Eve pauses, and looks at me intently. "According to your team's feedback, you have some weaknesses that challenge your beliefs."

"All right. So we sort out the truths of this mess, and I work on things. How do you know which ones strengthen my core?" I shake a finger at her. "And, don't tell me everything."

"Every leader, every person is different. Yet there is one set of truths that remain throughout all industries, all countries, and all leader styles."

I rap the table with my hands. "Drum roll..."

"Lean leader standard work."

Great. She wants me to be a quality jerk. Back in the 90s, we had total quality management, TQM, and then we had the Quality Office in the 2000s. No can do.

"What are you thinking?"

"I'm thinking about the Cold Miser." If I'm going down, I might as well have fun.

Eve has to think about that one. I don't know if she has children, but doesn't everyone know who the Cold Miser is?

"The Cold Miser. Lean leader standard work makes you think of the Cold Miser. This can't be good. Unless it's a dancing part."

"'No can do, Mrs. C.'" I shake my head. Eve waits for more. "Mrs. Claus asks the Cold Miser if he will let it snow in South Town, for just one day. The Cold Miser knows this is a huge request that will never, ever work because his brother the Heat Miser won't let it happen. 'Wait! Hollllld everything. No can do, Mrs. C.'"

Eve holds her head in her hands, and she is shaking. I think she is laughing. My coach has a soul, and a sense of humor.

"That is the…the most whacked out reaction I've had in a long time, Joel." Eve's laughter fills our little corner of the café.

"You're cracking already, and we've only met a few times." I am proud of my accomplishment. Gotta take the little victories at this point.

Eve collects herself. "Aw, Joel, why do you have to be a lean hater?"

I tell her the truth. I've survived too many total quality management efforts, too many quality office rules, regulations and processes. The quality jerks have nearly killed me, and a lot of other people, too. Lean is just another quality effort in the disguise of high end tools, with words that people like.

True to form, Eve asks me if I've ever had lean training. I haven't, but I've heard enough about it from my industry peers to know it. She's not satisfied that this is a good reason to hate lean.

"Don't try to tell me that after being a leader for 15 years that lean is going to turn me into an agile leader."

Eve smiles, "Tell me more."

"Lean is for manufacturers and hospitals, not for WL. We don't have a lot of repeatable processes."

More silence.

"I know how this ends. No can do, Mrs. Claus."

"Joel, can you give it a try? I'm not asking you to go to lean training. I'm asking you to look at your leadership with a new lens. The lens is lean leadership."

I say nothing. I am losing ground. Damn this coaching.

"You know what I think? You're objecting to something that you have no idea about it." Eve leans over the table. "Can you tell me what the five parts of lean leader standard work are?"

"No." I sneer. "I didn't have time to learn them because I have been too busy reviewing *quality* reports."

"Right. So if you can't even name one tenet of lean leader standard work, how can you say no to it?"

"It has the word *lean* in it, that's why."

We argue a while longer before Eve gives me an assignment. It feels a lot like giving in, but I did agree to try coaching with her. I owe our relationship that respect.

My breakthrough project, or assignment, is to research the lean leader standard work *go and see*. I think Eve was supposed to teach me this during our coaching time, but I pushed back for so long, we ran out of time.

Once I research what it means to *go and see*, I am to see if there are any connections to the team feedback. That damn feedback. I don't even want to look at it again, and now it's become part of my breakthrough project.

I leave the café completely exhausted. First the feedback, and now lean. It's officially all I can take for the day. Yet when I look at my calendar, I have a mess of one-on-ones scheduled. If I reschedule them all later this week, the domino effect will wreak havoc in new places. If I cancel them all together, I won't know what's going on. That will for sure come back to haunt me. I'm better off just keeping them on the books for today, and attending as a zombie.

If I can manage to stay awake during the meetings, I will be wondering if this is the person who thinks I am defensive. I'll be going through that damn list in my head instead of being a good listener. The faster I can get through this day the better. A run in the evening sun sounds good, but I won't have the energy. Agile, I mean, lean coaching is sucking the life right out of me.

Francie Van Wirkus

Clearing emails, I think about how much things have changed since I met Eve. It's only been a few weeks, and already she has come in to the heart of my territory, and gathered feedback about what kind of leader I am. If that's not disturbing and disruptive enough, she has forced me to change my relationship with Lora, which has been stagnant for a long time. Lora is the most dysfunctional leader ever to work at WL, and somehow I have to do the work to make our relationship better.

Reflections

My resources think I stink as a leader.

My managers think I stink as a leader.

My teams struggle to say anything good about me. Why else would they say I'm a nice dresser?!

Lean = Cold Miser = no can do.

Lean = quality jerk training.

Where is agile in this agile coaching?

I like my notebook.

Go & See

I don't think I actually recovered from my last meeting with Eve, but I did pull out of the exhaustion part of it. Once I did, I made time before a day full of meetings to begin my breakthrough project. Researching *go & see* was definitely opening Pandora's Box. So much information on what seemed to be a very trite thing. There were tons of companies, training, articles and books on the topic, but most of them looked pretty similar.

It's interesting that Eve didn't prescribe a specific website to visit. In fact, I'm surprised I wasn't handed a book that was published by her coaching firm. She left the research door wide open to my own interpretation. Must be part of her grand strategy. I told her I'd go along with it, and so I did my assignment. I wanted to keep it simple, so my notes from my research are short.

Go & See Research

The gemba (what is that?)

Respect for people (really, by visiting them at their desk?)

See how the process works.

See the obstacles and waste.

See the current state of things.

Coaching and mentoring on the job.

Now for the hard part: looking at the team's feedback and then finding connections to *go & see*. Fine. I don't know what gemba means, but I'm sure Eve will educate me.

I review the feedback. I can't find any connection to *go & see* in my strengths, but I think I find some in my weaknesses:

Francie Van Wirkus

Arrives late to meetings.
After arriving late for a meeting, jumps in right away, often
making us double back.
Access—hard to find him.
Access—hard to know if he is avoiding us or just buried.
Share more of your vision
Meet us for coffee or lunch.
We have tried to have lunch with them and were told they don't
have lunch with people at our level.

Reflections

Being more accessible to my teams will be hard. Booked solid daily.

Which is why I am late to some meetings. Too much going on!

My calendar is open to anyone; I'm not that hard to find.

I'm not hiding; I'm working on what I believe is the highest priority.

I would like to share more of my vision, if I knew what it was!

The team values time with me. This is encouraging.

I have so many required lunches to do stakeholdering and build
relationships. Am I supposed to ditch those in favor of my team?

Good enough. I'm sure Eve and I will dig right in at our next meeting. In the
meantime, I have to meet up with Lora to ask her about India. I'm *en fuego*.
I'm on fire.

Cold Miser

It's Thursday morning and J&L's café is hopping and upbeat. These cold, gloomy days need an elixir. I order my own, the house blend, and see Eve sitting in a different spot. That woman is full of curve balls. But she's never given me reason not to trust her. So I do. Even with this heavy, obnoxious feedback assignment. I hope she realizes how massive this is for me.

Our first order of business was talking about my meet up with Lora. Then, we were going to get into what Eve called the *crux* of her coaching. Great, there's more. Man, I thought we were knee deep in it already. But I trust her, so fine.

"So how did it go?" She asks.

I happily report that I completed my first step in the direction of building Lora's trust. I tell Eve how, after listening to her talk at great length about the shopping she did, and the places she ate dinner with our partners, we actually got to some substance. We talked about work.

"Well done, Joel."

"Thanks. It was just one meeting." I sigh. I know better. Eve will make me keep doing this forever. "You probably want me to do it again."

"Do *you* think you should do it again? Is there value in this time?"

"She seemed to appreciate me reaching out to her. But she is a narcissist, so any and all attention is good."

"I'm in counselor mode," Eve announces. "What makes you think Lora is a narcissist? Are you trained in psychotherapy?" She was honestly asking me.

"No." I smile. "I don't have to be trained to know that I'm dealing with someone who believes the world revolves around them. If you spent any time with her, you would notice it too. Everything comes back to her. Everything is about *her*. Also, my sister is married to one." I give her some of my favorite Lora one-liners and my reasons why it's narcissistic.

"I didn't know you were a runner." She knows nothing about my private life. And when it embarrasses her in a group setting that she doesn't know about

my private life, it is my fault. She expects me, well, all of us, to be interested in the things she has achieved, and what she has to say, but she's not at all interested in our achievements or what we have to say."

I'm getting more and more animated as I talk about Lora. My shoulders are tight and I'm destroying the java jacket that was around my cup. I am opening a part of me that has been buried. Safely tucked away so it doesn't ruin me. Things have been really bad, and I've just rolled over. So many years, days, and hours to feel this way, and not do anything about it. None of it can be good for my health or my personal growth. Have I even had any personal growth?! It doesn't feel good to talk about all of this with Eve, but it feels good that Eve is listening.

"I am surrounded." She's always saying that she's around people who just don't measure up to how good she is. She inserts herself in many things because she honestly believes that without her advice or direction, people will not know what to do.

"Do you need more examples?" I'm *en fuego* again.

"Nope." Eve's face is tense. "You were very clear." She pauses, looking like she needs to collect herself.

Eve changes gears to get into the crux of her coaching: to work with my inner caveman. All righty then. It sounds remarkably like the human psychology terms *id* and *ego, which* I learned about so very long ago. Apparently each of us has an inner caveman, who is only interested in the here and now. This inner caveman holds us back from change of all kinds.

Eve used the example of trying to lose weight. You want to do it. You may have even had a doctor or specialist tell you that you need to do it, or you will get sick. So you work out a plan. You go to the store to buy healthy food. But you shopped after work, when you were really hungry. Shopping cart full of good things, you can't help but drive past the chips aisle. Before you know it, the two-for-six-dollars chip sale is in your cart. They are opened in the car on the way home...

I just need to try harder, you say. *I am weak, and I'm bad for being weak. I have to try harder...*

You want to start working out again before work. This goes well for the first two days. But then there is a cold snap, and it's minus five degrees. You don't want to get up in the dark and cold, so you sleep in. Then, you're mad at yourself all day for not getting up and going out. *I just need to work harder at getting up...*

Eve instructs that the inner caveman in each of us does not like to be uncomfortable in any way. The caveman doesn't like being hungry or eating healthy food, being too cold, too hot, too wet, or too dry; being left out, embarrassed, rushed, or put on the spot. We humans like things in the comfort zone. I can definitely buy into that.

Trying harder, wanting it more, or beating yourself up mentally about your failure will not work for most people because our immediate needs win out over long term needs. What you want or need right now is most important. I can buy into that too. When you want pizza, you just want pizza.

It's poorly understood by most people, including me, I guess. It's the reason there are so many magazine articles, books, and programs to buy to lose weight, speak a foreign language, cook healthy, or train for that marathon. It's also what fuels a lot of those social media platitude posters - you know, the *because I want it more* messages.

Eve explains to me that our inner caveman is so powerful, even the best laid plans with professional coaching crumble apart in a heartbeat. She says there is a way to work *with* your inner caveman. Trying to outsmart him won't work. Ignoring him won't work either. Work *with* him, because he's not going away. In case you are wondering, yes, Lora has an inner cave*woman*. That concept is the foundation for the coaching I'm going to experience. She assures me once again that we will get to agile leadership...

"How did your reflection assignment work out with *go & see*?"

I tell her there is a ton of information out there on the topic, and that it's hard to know which sources are credible and which are not. Like hiking in the Grand Canyon, how to know what is the best way? I pull out my list of learning from my research and share it with her:

Go & See Research

The gemba (what is that, really?)

Respect for people (really, by visiting them at their desk?)

See how the process works.

See the obstacles and waste.

See the current state of things.

Coaching and mentoring on the job.

Eve doesn't read it yet. She was focused on my story. "Did you see radically different ideas or examples of *go & see*?"

I had to stop and think. "I'm not sure, because I didn't read many of them. I probably skimmed three or four web pages to come up with my research."

"Fair enough." Eve leans back in her café chair. "Joel, thank you for doing this assignment. You went from 'no can do, Mrs. C.' to researching three or four websites. That's terrific progress."

I shrug. "Doesn't mean I'm in your corner on this."

"Well aware, Joel." Eve's eyes are dancing. She can't wait to get me to like lean leader standard work. She looks at my list. "Would you like to talk about the concept of *gemba*?"

"I'm not a very good dancer," I chided.

"Right." Eve looks at me, still waiting for an answer.

"Yes," I breathe, "please tell me more about the concept of gemba." I'm already tired from this session.

Eve pauses. There are so many pauses, and yet for each one I am grateful. It's like being out for a hard run, and stopping to rest. I'm certain that rest is as much for her as it is for me.

"Let's stop here, Joel. I'm giving you another assignment, and then we're done for today. You look exhausted."

"I'm all right." I try to perk up.

"We're stopping here. Ready?"

I throw in the towel. "Lay it on me."

"Before our next session, research the Japanese word *gemba*. Nothing else. Make a few notes, just like you did here. Then write down where you think your gemba is."

I blink. I don't *want* to stop, but I don't want to keep going, either. I'm researching Japanese words. She's turning me into a quality jerk, I just know it.

"Joel?"

"Sorry…yes, got the assignment. Gemba, it is."

Reflections

Things have been really bad, and I have just rolled over and done nothing about it.

I have been asleep at my job; so many things bother me, yet I do nothing about them.

Lora is a narcissist and it impacts me and my team.

I have an inner caveman who wants satisfaction RIGHT NOW!

Gemba is a huge topic. Lots of quality jerks out there.

Where is the agile in this agile coaching?

Francie Van Wirkus

Ideas for Sale

It's my monthly career development meeting with Lora. It's different than my weekly one-on-one meetings, and different than our weekly status meeting.

WL has a career development process and template for directors to use, but we rarely talk about it. Except for at the end of the year, when I have to give it to Lora, and she has to report that she's worked on it with me. So I make sure I keep my template current and in the filing cabinet.

I dread these meetings, because they are never about my career development. In fact, they are never about me. They usually begin about me, but within 10 minutes, Lora is doing all the talking. What starts as a vanilla question or statement quickly becomes an elaborate set of white board drawings that must be photographed on a smart phone for posterity. Today is no different than any of the previous career development meetings.

Twenty minutes into the meeting, and Lora is in full-blown, four color dry erase marker-strategy mode. She asks me what I think an agile community of practice would look like at WL. I share my thoughts with her, including a few marketing ideas to get membership going and to sustain it. When talking about how complicated it is to change things at WL, I use an analogy of Vienna torte. Many layers, rich and complex. I offer a few more thoughts, because we are casually speaking, right?

Wrong.

The next day, Lora is presenting to a large group of stakeholders at a steering committee meeting. My ideas were presented to the group as her ideas. Well, she presented them in the absence of my name or input. In fact, she used my damn Vienna torte analogy. She changed it slightly, calling the complicated situation "full of layers like a French pastry." God.

I spent the rest of that meeting trying not to vomit right on the conference table. How can she do that without any conscience, any acknowledgement that someone else gave her inspiration?

It disgusted me, but it didn't surprise me. Lora steals my ideas, and repackages them as her own all of the time. She also pillages Meryll's ideas.

I'm sure she stole some from Jack when she interviewed him for the job. Although, the pastry analogy was over the top obvious. I have called her on it in the past, but she never admits to stealing from me. She claims she got input from me on her ideas, and she made them better (because no one is as good as she is). No, definitely not worth arguing with her about this one. But, we did have a career development meeting...

Not long ago, I was happy, even complacent with my job and with WL. I had ridiculous assignments and goals that could never be reached, but missing them only made me want more. I've never liked working for Lora or Rick, but up until now, I'm beginning to think I've been asleep at the wheel. Meeting with Eve is beginning to shine light on places that have been stifled, packed away, or ignored. It's beyond uncomfortable, it's disturbing. At the same time, this disturbance is giving me energy. I can't define it yet, but it feels like it could be a good thing.

Driving home that evening, I think about my quality jerk assignment from Eve. Gemba. It doesn't even sound good. Still, I need to get cracking on it, so I don't disappoint Eve.

Reflections

I used to think I was happy at work. I was wrong.

Still think lean is for quality jerks.

Francie Van Wirkus

The Gemba

Eve's assignment was to research the Japanese word *gemba,* make a few notes, and then write down where I think my gemba is. Though it still really bothers me, I resist the temptation to look at the feedback from my teams again. I research gemba, and once again find a grand canyon of information. Thank you, Google.

Gemba, genba -Japanese for the real place.

Gembutsu-Japanese for the real thing.

Used for business process improvement (AKA quality jerks).

Any place in an organization where humans add value.

My gemba is my desk.

That wasn't so bad. The topic looks a little heavier than Eve made it out to be. There are books, training sessions, webinars, blogs and case studies. I'm happy to stick with my short assignment and let Eve lead me through the rest.

"Nice work on your breakthrough project, Joel."

"Thank you. It wasn't that difficult."

Eve winks. "When I gave you the assignment, you acted like I was asking you to change religions."

"Yeah, yeah. Just because I did the assignment doesn't mean I like it or agree with it."

"If you're not careful, I may have to send you out to paint a fence."

"Nice." I'm more negative about this lean thing by the moment.

"So let's learn about gemba by talking about *your* gemba, Joel. Where is it?"

"My gemba is my desk. Sometimes it's a conference room, sometimes it's a phone conference."

"Do you build things on your desk?"

"Uh…on my laptop, so yeah, I guess I do."

"Could someone look at your desk, and see the value you add to WL?"

"Huh." I pause. I thought I had nailed the assignment. "If the gemba is the actual place where value is added, and I have an office to work in…"

"But where is the value, Joel? If I walk into your office right now, I won't see anything but a desk, maybe a laptop and a few personal effects. I won't see what it is you do to add value for WL."

"That's because it's in my head."

"Knowledge worker."

"Yes, I am a knowledge worker."

"Right, so your gemba is…?"

"My gemba is in my head," I announce. "I guess you could also argue that it's in the places where I engage my head, like my laptop, meetings, and interactions with others."

"Right. The actual place where you add value is your gemba."

"But unlike manufacturing, someone could come to a team meeting or observe my interaction with others, and have a hard time knowing if I'm working on the right thing, or anything at all."

"Great observations, Joel." Eve smiles. "Gemba is a rich topic, and if you continue with our coaching, you will find the answers to those questions in your work. But what I want to do now is turn back to the feedback from your teams."

"If we must."

"We must. The feedback is very telling, and it connects well to becoming an agile leader. But please don't think we are going to work on every single thing on this list. The feedback is not positioned over and above the vision you built."

"Got it."

"Can you please take out your notes? The ones on how your gemba research might connect to some of the feedback?"

I pull out my notes.

"Let's take a look at the first one, Joel. Actually, those first two. They look very connected."

We both read the feedback and my notes:

Feedback: Arrives late to meetings.

Being more accessible to my teams will be hard. Booked solid daily.

Feedback: After arriving late for a meeting, jumps in right away, often making us double back.

Which is why I am late to some meetings. Too much going on!

Eve tells me that she could just instruct me to never be late to meetings, but she says I would be missing the point. I push back on how booked my calendar is. I tell Eve she has no idea what kind of pressure I'm under to be a director in this area. Eve says she completely gets it, but that we are only as booked for meetings as we want to be.

"It's an exercise in futility, Eve. This feedback tells me they don't like me, so why would I bust my butt to show up and be with them?"

"Your teams are asking that you be more present with them. If they hated you, they wouldn't request that you be around at all."

"But they say I jump in and interrupt them."

"Why do you do that?"

"Because I'm late! Don't you see? I'm running from one place to the next, one gemba to the next, so when I do arrive there, I feel I have to be rather spontaneous with what I'm thinking. If I don't share with them my thoughts at that moment, later on might be too late."

"Okay," Eve finished her matcha latte. "Let's say you can't help but be late for a meeting. It happens. What would be the harm in just folding into the meeting, without saying anything, as a leader at the gemba?"

"Um, you mean walk in, and just say nothing?"

Then, Eve's question smacks me between the eyes. "Don't you hate it when Lora dominates every one and every meeting?"

"Man." I put my head in my hands. I'm becoming Lora! "Ugh, this feels terrible."

"I'm not asking you to go to a meeting and say nothing. But when you arrive late to a meeting, there is no urgency for you to do anything but silently become part of the group."

"For how long? What if there is a really good point that needs my interpretation?"

"Relax, Joel. This is a rich topic. But let's try to keep it simple and impactful. Use this rule: for however late you are, you must not speak in the meeting for the same amount of time." Eve meets my blank stare. "So, if you are 15 minutes late to the meeting, no talking for 15 minutes. Even then, work in slowly."

"But--"

"Remember how much effort went into hiring your managers and their teams? You hired a ton of quality, talented people."

"Yes, we did."

"Here's a curious thing. Most leaders find that when they have a burning thought, one that gives them the urge to interrupt and share it…" Eve pauses for my attention. "When they wait five minutes, someone else on the team usually comes up with the same idea."

"So, what *can* I say?"

Eve puts up a hand. "Lots, Joel. But you don't have to prove your worth in every gemba, at every moment."

"But…"

"Your presence doesn't have to be validated with words."

I put my head in my hands again. She's right. I'm validating my presence. I race to get to a meeting, walk in late, and then speak up as soon as I can to make sure people in the meeting know that I care about what is being discussed. I want to look engaged. It's how I work for most meetings, no matter if they are my peers or my resources. I never think about the fact that what I'm saying or the question I'm asking might have already been discussed. I must come off as a real jerk. Ugh.

But, what about meetings with other directors, and with Lora? There is a lot of pontificating going on in those meetings; if I'm not one of the gang, I could get left out. Or people will think I'm pissed and accuse me of holding back on them. Then I'll get nailed for not being a team player. This does not feel good.

"Is it the same for meetings with peers? People might think I'm weak or inattentive."

"I saw it on your face, Joel. You know the answer."

I sigh. "Yeah, but there are different dynamics when it's a meeting with my peers or with Lora."

Eve said it doesn't matter the venue. The kind of leader she is coaching me to be is secure enough in their role to remain silent in an entire meeting, any meeting, with any players, if that is what's needed. She said that my inner caveman has a lot to do with this behavior. Great, I am late for meetings and I interrupt people because I AM a caveman. Where's my club…

"This is going to be hard. I feel like I don't have the entire picture."

"You don't have the entire picture. It's too much to absorb all at once. Lean leader standard work is a lot of things. We are working on *go & see*. Notice it doesn't say *go & talk*."

"You're turning me into the strong, silent type?"

"On occasion, yes. Overall, no. I'm going to turn you into an agile leader, who knows his purpose and how he adds value. Once you know your purpose, you will know what questions to ask at the gemba of your teams. Even when you're late."

I told Eve that sounded great, but none of this solves the fact that I'm over booked, and stressed out from being over booked. That's when I got my next breakthrough assignment: to review my gemba. I am to print my schedule for each day, and then review it at the end of each day. I have to write a note about how I added value in each of the meetings or events. Even if it's a meeting with Lora or Rick or my peers. I think I know where she's going with this assignment.

Then, as extra credit, I can go back and color code the ones that add value, and the ones that don't. We'll use the color-coded calendar for our next discussion. I've always wanted to change my calendar, and be more protective of my time, but our culture here doesn't allow for that.

I'm a director; we are not expected to have a life. We are supposed to be needed nonstop, all day long. In fact, most of my personal vision is completely counter to WL culture. There might be sluggish work going on in the lower ranks, but not with the director team. We are where it's at.

"What about that other feedback item? The one that I'm hard to find? Won't missing these meetings make that worse? Or is that one that we're going to ignore?"

"Let's say you learn that you attend some meetings where you don't add value. Let's say, hypothetically, of course, that you stop attending those meetings where you don't add value. If you're not in wasteful meetings, what do you think you could be doing?"

"Um, more research?"

"Maybe. Where will you do that research?"

"At my gemba?" I have no idea. I'm tired.

"Possibly. But you hired all of these great people, and they hired great people, too. Do you think they might be able to help you?"

Ding! I chuckle, and feel the heat of embarrassment roll up my back. "I get it. If I research with my teams and resources, I will learn something, and they will have more access to me."

Eve is pleased with the breakthrough of my thick-headedness.

It all sounds good, but it's just not that simple at WL. Lora and Rick are not going to make this easy. I quickly thought of Jack and Meryll. Will they have the same assignment? Maybe the three of us could power up together, and make a plan. Safety in numbers.

"So if I suddenly begin to cancel out of meetings, I can't just say it's a coaching assignment."

"Why not?"

"Because WL doesn't work that way. Our culture expects that I'm going to be overbooked."

"Like an airline knowingly overbooking a flight."

"Exactly. You know it's not right, but you take your chances and usually end up on the upswing."

"Do you...end up on the upswing?"

This was so exasperating. "No."

"How is culture going to change if one leader in the company can't?"

"You took the words right out of my mouth."

Eve pauses, and I enjoy my rest.

"Let's do a five whys exercise, Joel, so we can dismantle this. Why don't you like this assignment?"

"It's counter culture to being a director at WL."

"Why do you think you can't be the first one to change your calendar?"

"Because the company's transformation doesn't depend solely on me."

"Why don't you think you are a change leader?"

"I am, but more importantly, I need my job."

"Why do you think you'll get fired for doing your coaching assignment? Lora and Rick are the ones who sent you here, remember?"

"Because they say one thing and do another. She will say it's safe to change, but I know the reality of her demands. And Rick, he's down in the weeds with us, in those one-on-ones. They say they want agile, but I don't want to be the one who's fired, demoted or ostracized because they found out they really don't want to be agile."

"Why do you think they don't trust the coaching process?"

"Past performance is the best indicator of future outcomes."

Eve pauses again. I enjoy yet another rest. I feel like I wrestled her five whys technique to the ground. Victory over lean! Until she speaks.

"Thank you, Joel. We dismantled that one quickly. It goes back to trust, doesn't it?"

Boom. "Yes ma'am."

Eve tells me she's grappling with how to pave the way for change with this assignment. She considers calling Lora and Rick herself to tell them of the assignment, but she lands on having me do it. Either way, I hate the idea of broadcasting my calendar changes. I don't want her contacting my leaders like I can't speak for myself, but I don't want to approach them on this either. Eve stresses she doesn't want to be my enabler, and that she believes it is for the best if I do it. I know she's right, but none of it feels good to me. It feels like huge risk for which the fallout might not happen for months, perhaps long after Eve has moved on.

"I believe in you, Joel. This is a big assignment, and I respect you a ton for taking it on."

"Thanks." I lie.

"I don't think it's too early in our coaching program to give you this assignment. I think you might be shocked when you begin to really look at how you are spending your time. Don't forget to color code the meetings where you add value or get value, and the ones that are waste. Take a photo of it, or a screen print. I don't care about the content of the photo, but I do care about seeing what kind of picture you colored. If you can take notes about why you coded things you did, even better. Next, take yourself out of the ones that don't add any value for you."

Eve gives me some ideas of what kind of language I can use to cancel with each meeting organizer, such as *"I am focusing my time where I am needed most, so I won't be attending this meeting. Please contact me if you have questions..."* Choosing the words isn't the problem, as we discovered in the five whys exercise. It's trusting that I can actually pull this off.

"Get your assistant Marilyn involved. We're not just going to do this for one week, Joel." Eve warns me.

"I figured so much." I try to picture life on the other side of this assignment. "If I'm going to be a pioneer, blazing the trail of having a sane schedule, I want to be able to enjoy my hard work."

Eve's eyes are sparkling. She's up to something. God, please no more.

"Joel, the cool thing about being the pioneer is that other people will see what you are doing, and be disturbed, and then they will be inspired, and then they will be doing what they saw you do. It's working in your organization right now, with distrust and waste, but it can be used for good. This calendar assignment might be the very first of its kind."

"...since 1995."

Eve laughs. But really, she's giving me good advice. I'm trying to get my head around what this is, but because I have a team of managers, I need to think of them, too. I shouldn't be surprised when my managers mirror the same behavior. I try to imagine what that might look like. Some of that will be good. There might be a few managers who will take advantage…never mind. I can't speculate about the future. I have to focus on what's in front of me right now.

Now I know what that sparkle in her eyes was all about. Exponential change. At least, the potential for it.

"Now, about that inner caveman of yours, Joel. He's going to find 100 reasons why you should avoid this conversation. We know some of the other things you want, so let's use one of them to indulge you for doing this breakthrough project."

"Like, I get a belt of whiskey when it's over?" I couldn't resist.

"Nope. Look at your list of personal wants. I want to begin to weave those into your days. What's going on with quality workouts and Ironman Boulder 2017?"

"Nothing right now. How does doing work become a reward?"

"You said that quality workouts and doing Ironman Boulder 2017 would be energizing and exciting to you, remember? These are things you really, really want." Eve tilts her head. "Of course your vision is entitled to change…has it?"

"No. I'm just trying to understand the coaching process."

"Leave that to me, Joel. Stop trying to outsmart, out-argue, or out-maneuver a proven coaching process, and just trust me. Stop wrestling for control."

I sigh. She sees right through my questions, and it's annoying. Because she is right, and because I don't like being weak in any way. But here I am, letting another layer of myself be peeled away, in the name of improvement.

I tell Eve about last year, when I finished two half Ironmans, and really enjoyed myself. After that great experience, I wanted to race an Ironman. And Boulder seems to be the perfect one, practically in my back yard. I don't want to do the race just to do it; I want to do it well, so I researched different Ironman coaches. I got a few names and recommendations, but I didn't hire one. Then I got distracted with work. That's nothing new.

"It bothers me that I just dropped that idea. I was ready to make a change, and then it just got sucked away by work. Once I can get a better grip on what we are doing here, I would like to hire one."

Eve smiles, but she calls me out, "There you go again, trying to *get a grip on coaching.*"

"Fine. Once I am more comfortable with this coaching arrangement, I would like to begin working with an Ironman coach. That will really make my goal real. And it will be very exciting."

"So how about this, Joel: you follow through with your calendar assignment, you get to hire an Ironman coach, and can begin in a month or two."

"I like it."

"Something tells me you will have time on your calendar to enjoy the fruits of your work here. I can't wait to hear about it."

I walk to work exhausted again. Yet there is this shiver of excitement in the air. I'm too paralyzed and overwhelmed to do anything about it but admire it from afar.

Back at WL, I walk straight to Marilyn's desk after our meeting, and tell her of my calendar overhaul plan. She knew I was getting leadership coaching, so it was easy to share the basics of the gemba and how I'm going to spend more time with my teams. She's a smart, driven woman who can make all kinds of magic happen, so she was ready to dive in and do the calendar work for me. No, I tell her, I need to do this exercise so I learn about my work.

"Let me get this straight." Marilyn leans her large body over her desk. She's been here 25 years, and has seen it all come and go. "I am no longer the keeper of your calendar?"

"You still are the keeper of it. Just let me color code stuff, and don't be surprised if you see me cancel meetings and instead have time with my teams, noted as *gemba*."

"Right, gemba," she smiles, with 25 years of experience knowing not to take me or this calendar project too seriously.

"This is really an honest effort, Marilyn. It's all me, not a corporate mandate of any kind. I want to be better for my teams, and my family. I want to get home by 5:30 p.m. And the kids have all kinds of events that I've only been able to see parts of, or missed completely."

She puffs her cheeks. "Oh, I remember how sad you were at Christmas time when you missed Cici's concert."

"That's what I'm talking about! Cici's already five years old. She's growing up so fast. I'm just—"

Marilyn puts a hand up, "I understand, Joel. Just tell me how I can help you, and I will be happy to do it."

"Thanks. I don't know exactly what I need yet, but I will share with you as I learn."

She shakes her head and smiles. "Don't give up the fight to see your kids grow up."

"That and my sanity."

Francie Van Wirkus

Reflections

Gemba is far more complicated than I imagined.

There is hope for my calendar. My life.

Filling the gaps I make in my calendar will not be hard.

I don't like being the first to change.

I am more worried about the status of my job than I thought.

I can't wait to get an Ironman coach!

Seeing Red

"Oh my. Would you look at all that red," Meryll gushes. She and Jack are looking over my shoulder at my newly color-coded calendar.

"At first I thought I went too far, you know, just tagging meetings that I don't like as wasteful. Maybe I had a bad day or a bad attitude," I say. "But I left it alone, and came back to it the next day with no different results."

"That's so cool," Jack smiles. "I can't wait to do this to my calendar. I wish I would have done this when I first started here. Everyone added me to every meeting, and since then, I've just sort of kept them."

"So that's why you showed this to us? To get us to try it?" Meryll had doubt in her voice. I was sure she was thinking about the pushback.

"Yes. More importantly, I need help with the communication around changing my calendar."

Meryll sighed. "Uh-huh."

"We all know that *uh-huh.*" Jack warns. "She's got doubts."

"You can't just turn your calendar on its head, Joel. You can't just dump all these meetings. The people who own these meetings will freak. And without you there, they won't get any work done. There will be chaos, and it will be tracked back to you. Then, Lora and Rick will catch wind of it and freak out too. No win situation." Meryll shakes her head *no.*

Jack points a thumb at Meryll. "Mournful Meryll, here."

"No, think about it Jack. You are a director. You can't just stop showing up like that. Our culture won't allow for it. You'll get dinged for it, ostracized for it, maybe even fired for it," Meryll sighs. "I care about you two, and don't want you to lose your job."

"I am already miserable," I say. "Because of this damn calendar. Even Marilyn wants to help."

Meryll rolls her eyes. "My coach isn't making me do anything dumb like that."

"I'm so fragmented, Meryll. I'm looking to get the waste out of my day."

"Right." Jack's eyes are lit. Things are clicking easily for him because he doesn't have 15-20 years of culture holding him back like Meryll does.

I tell them about my *five whys* conversation with Eve. It's hard to do, because I haven't quite digested everything myself, but it felt right. I surprised myself in the way I talked with them like I loved the assignment. Just a day ago, I was resisting it with all I was made of. I was scared. Today, I'm still scared, but I'm ready to try it.

"I'm ready for change. I'm so ready that I'm willing to put it on the line, take the heat, whatever. Maybe our teams will miss us, and I'll have to fold back into the meetings. Maybe I'll just be needed once in a while. Maybe they will ride off into the sunset without me and not think twice. It's unknown, but totally worth a try. I won't hold it against you if you don't join me. But if you do join me, I promise to give you all the support I can. We will be a team on this."

Meryll put a hand up, "But--"

"I fully expect it to be hard and uncomfortable, and a lot of other stuff that I haven't even thought through yet. It's not going to be perfect. It *is* going to be better."

"Ohhh," Jack's eyes widened, "I am *so* in. I've only been here six months, but I haven't been able to take a day off from work yet. I feel like I'm on a treadmill that never stops."

I tilt my head toward Jack, and say to Meryll, "We don't remember it now, but that was us 15 years ago. So eager to please, to lead, that we allowed ourselves to get completely trampled."

"Okay, so we have better calendars with more time. What is it we are supposed to be doing with this time? What does an agile leader do all day?"

I tell Meryll I'm studying *gemba*. Right now, I'm interested in filling the gaps of my time with my coach, and with learning about gemba.

"That's not agile. That's lean." Meryll objects.

"Lagile?" Jack offers.

"Seriously, what the hell is your coach teaching you? Lean is lean, agile is agile."

"Whoa. Is that what you've learned so far?" Jack is full of drama.

"I can't believe you two," she sighs. "Japanese words and colored calendars. I don't like where we're headed."

Time to level with Meryll. "I know you're miserable, Meryll. You can pretend you love your job and the miniscule amount of *work-life balance* you have." I hold up my fingers like quotation marks. "But the truth is, you've repressed your displeasure. You have a ton of resentment for the way your WL career has unfolded."

"I don't like to think about it." She is quiet.

"I know. I didn't end up with this breakthrough project by choice. My coach forced me to go there in our session. I had no idea how many things I have repressed about my job as a director, and about working for WL. It's really uncomfortable thinking about them, but I am ready for change. And, I don't care if it's a lean thing or an agile thing. I'm making it *my* thing."

"American flag flapping in the wind behind him..." Jack adds color whenever he can.

"Fine!" Meryll cracked. Yes!

Meryll, Jack and I plan how, with Marilyn's help, we are going to communicate to our meeting owners, teams, and Lora and Rick. We planned for consistency across all meeting owners, and special words about this being a coaching assignment for Lora and Rick. We also planned to meet every Friday to set up our calendars for the next week. We don't think we'll have to review each other's calendars forever, but it is good practice right now.

I was so glad Meryll jumped in to join us. I knew she wouldn't be able to stand being left out of this monumental change.

Francie Van Wirkus

Originally, I was going to wait until tomorrow to take action. But then I was so wound up after talking with Meryll and Jack that I began making calls. It wasn't that hard. Once I stumbled through the language on the first call, I was much more comfortable. I'm sure I messed something up, but overall, I got the job done.

The reaction was mostly neutral or positive. That's not a good barometer, though, because I think most resources wouldn't give me negative feedback. One project manager, however, did ask a few questions.

"So, you're not moving on to another assignment, and you're staying as sponsor of this project, but you're not going to call in for the weekly status?"

"That's right. Your team can work through the status without me. If there are times when you want me to share insight with you on a specific topic, I'm happy to drop in as a guest."

"Can I ask why you are doing this? Is it something in the way I am running the project?"

"I assure you, it's not about how you run the project. I am making this change to better focus on where I can add the most value."

And so it went. In the end, the project manager said he understood, but I don't think he trusted me. I imagine he fully expects to be pulled off the project, and sent to a less desirable assignment.

Now for the hard part: Lora and Rick. Meryll and Jack wanted to join me, so I invited all of them to my one-on-one with Rick. I told Rick ahead of time that we would have guests at our status, and he was agreeable to it.

Once we were all together, I didn't waste any time talking about my breakthrough project from Eve. Just dive in. If for no other reason, to keep Lora from derailing the meeting. Jack and Meryll are letting me do all of the talking. I describe the exercise of color coding my calendar, and how I discussed where I add value with Meryll and Jack. Meryll and Jack are sound supporters, chiming in on occasion. Lora is physically straining not to speak.

"Are you three asking me if you can do this?" Rick checks his watch. How ironic.

"No." I say as neutral as I can. "We are sharing what we're doing, so you understand our motives and can support us. We feel this type of change might ruffle some feathers, so we wanted you to hear it from us first."

Rick nods his head. "Go ahead and give it a whirl." He has a faint smile. "Maybe I can glean something from your experience for my calendar."

"I love the idea!" Lora gushes. Great. She has a shiny, new toy with no clue how to use it. "I think I'm going to color code my calendar too. Have you seen that TED Talks video about that woman who..."

That's when Lora took over the room. Fortunately, Rick cut her short. He had to leave because he was double booked during our meeting time. If I hadn't invited special guests, our one-on-one would have been canceled or rescheduled to yet another inconvenient time.

"That was weird." Meryll sighs. "Lora is going to try it. How cool is that?"

"She's not going to try it, Meryll."

"What do you mean, Joel? You just heard her say it."

"Lora said she was going to color code her calendar," Jack sighs, "not *fix* her calendar."

"Ohhh." Meryll is mad at herself for not catching this nuance.

"She stripped out the meaning of the exercise and went right to the tool," I say.

Jack rolls his eyes. "Hammer and nail."

"Okay, so we didn't expect her to do it with us anyway," Meryll says. "I still feel great that we talked with them as a team, and got Rick's buy-in as a team."

I'm not sure where all of this landed. "I feel great and nervous all at once."

"That makes two of us," Jack adds.

Francie Van Wirkus

Reflections

We are leading others even when we are not ready or don't want to.

People at WL love new tools. They don't have time for a mindset change.

Out of the Box

Eve and I tuck into a window seat at J&L's Café. She asks me about my breakthrough project, and I gush about my accomplishment. From making the phone calls to the meeting with Rick and Lora with all five of us there, I was very pleased with leading this change. I know I'm not out of the woods yet, but so far, I haven't had any backlash. I'm pretty sure Lora didn't listen well enough to what I was saying to fully understand what I'm doing, so I'll probably have to circle back with her a few times.

"Excellent work, Joel. I love how you took the assignment a step further, and involved Meryll and Jack. Did you call that Ironman coach?"

"Yes." I bask in the accomplishment. "We are going to start up in two months. I can't wait."

"Love it." Eve pulls out her folder with the dreaded feedback from hell in it. She invites me to open my notebook to the reflection work I did on my gemba. "We are going to build on what we talked about last time. We have some good lessons in this feedback on how to connect it all. There is a lot more to build upon, and we are going to chip away at it until you have the full picture."

I open to my notes:

Feedback: Arrives late to meetings.

Being more accessible to my teams will be hard. Booked solid daily.

Feedback: After arriving late for a meeting, jumps in right away, often making us double back.

Which is why I am late to some meetings. Too much going on!

Feedback: Access—hard to find him,

My calendar is open to anyone; I'm not that hard to find.

Feedback: Access—hard to know if he is avoiding us or just buried.

I'm not hiding; I'm working on what I believe is the highest priority.

Feedback: Share more of your vision.

I would like to share more of my vision if I knew what it was!

Feedback: Meet us for coffee or lunch.

The team values time with me. This is encouraging.

Feedback: We have tried to have lunch with them and were told they don't have lunch with people at our level.

I have so many scheduled, required lunches to do stakeholdering and build relationships. Am I supposed to ditch those in favor of my team?

"Joel, now that you know where your gemba is, can you tell me where your manager's gemba is?"

"It's where they add value at WL, mostly in interactions with resources and other managers."

Eve has a slight wince but recovers quickly. What was that about? "Right. So where are the gembas of your teams?"

"At their desks, in meetings, wherever they are adding value to the work we are doing."

"Great. So when I tell you to use some of the newfound gaps in your calendar to *go & see*, what does that look like?"

"You led me right into it." I smile. I look at my feedback and notes. "I should be spending time with my managers and resources in different ways. But…I'm sure I'm going to mess it up."

"Nah. You're going to be great. That's because I have some can't-fail questions for you to ask in any gemba. You know there is a ton of information on gemba, and well, there are a ton of different gemba questions to ask. There are nuances to the questions; try not to get caught up in that right now. Our goal right now is to understand why you are asking these questions, and what to do with the answers. You can refine your questions over time. I want you to write them as I ask you, so you can begin to internalize them."

"Important questions, huh?"

"I assure you, once you learn how to use them, you will want to use them until the end of time. They are that good."

I write them:

What are you trying to do?

What have you tried so far?

How do you know it is working?

Eve tells me these are powerful questions because they are open ended. "You are not asking them in order to get a correct answer. You are asking to understand. Active listening is a huge part of this work." Eve suggests writing down what I learn on my iPad or a sticky note. I can handle that.

"One behavior *go & see* demands is that you get out of your office, and talk with your mangers and teams. Notice I didn't say management by walking around. This is about getting out and engaging your people. All of them. Too many leaders at your level get boxed into their office with marathon meetings. And, I know a few too many leaders at your level who are hiding out in their office." Eve winks.

"Hey, that's not me!"

"I know. And I believe you need time to yourself, but look at your feedback, Joel. People want to see you, and they need you. Teams want to see their leaders." Eve's really jazzed. "Every year, I help new organizations. I'm always mystified by how many companies still have giant cubie farms and important people offices and restricted conference rooms that are only for leaders. These are physical barriers to high performing teams that create social and political barriers."

I'm thinking about...*everything*. "I'm on board with it. But, how can I get a good view of what's going on. Their gemba is in their heads, remember?"

Eve tells me walking the gemba won't reveal everything I need to know, but taking a structured, focused approach to my time will help me better understand what I can't see. I'm going to have to trust her on this one.

She says my job is not to look for problems to fix or manage. I disagree. "Isn't that what I'm being paid to do?"

"Maybe, but it's not what you're being coached to do." Eve leans over the table. "You are a *director*, Joel. I am teaching you to become a *leader*. An agile leader."

"So, who is that? What is that?"

Eve smiles. She's not wearing lipstick today. "You're not going to get a recipe from me, so stop that path in your mind right now."

I sigh. "No recipe; how do I learn, YouTube?"

She sighs. We are wearing ourselves out. "Okay, I'll give you a little bit of a recipe." She pulls her chair in square to the table. Now I'm in for it...

Eve tells me she believes my leadership style to be command and control, and the culture of WL is the same. I don't argue that, but we're so big, don't we need organization like this? Eve tells me it's not about getting rid of managers and directors, but about getting them to focus on the right thing. The right thing begins with lean leadership, and builds from there.

"You keep talking about lean. When are you going to connect it to agile for me?"

"I will. And when I do, you will no longer care which one is which. Just that you are focused on the right things."

"All righty..."

"The best way for you to know the difference between command and control, and being an agile leader, is to begin using your new blocks of time for connecting with your teams. It's going to be awkward at first, but I know you can step past it, and begin making real connections."

"Right, a little awkward but I have the three questions."

"Right." Eve smiles. "Just don't read them. Always think about your intent." She types a few notes on my breakthrough project template. "Your assignment this week is to keep working on changing what your day looks like. Step one was looking for waste in your day," Eve grins. "I am still so very pleased with your last breakthrough project. That was great."

"Thank you." I'm doing something right.

"Now that you have these gaps, I want you to use some of them to go & see. This is going to be your new world."

"Okay, I will fill all the gaps with spending time with my teams."

"Not all of your time, Joel. You need to leave some open for reflection and learning. Time for you."

"How's that going to go over?" I'm skeptical, for a lot of reasons.

"It's not like you're sitting around smoking weed in your office."

"Someone at WL probably is, but it's not me."

"You're gonna be an Ironman!"

"Yes, I am."

"Reflection and learning happen in down time, not in gridlock. Like Ironman training, you can't keep piling on bike, run and swim workouts on top of each other without rest. Well, you can, but your performance will suffer, because your body needs time to soak in the work that's been done."

"So, you're an Ironman coach, too?"

"No. But I've finished five Ironmans."

"Five full Ironmans?"

Eve winces. "Ugh, I can't stand it when people use the term *full* Ironman. If I meant half, I would have said half. But I didn't. I said Ironman."

"Okay, okay, got it, Ironman Lady."

"I want to share another example from a company called Modus Cooperandi, because this is a really important topic that will connect up to others. Regarding your calendar not being 100 percent booked, think about it like a five lane freeway: when it's 50 percent full, the cars are moving pretty well, but when it's 90 percent full, things are not moving well. You don't want to be on the freeway at all if it's 100 percent full."

"Gridlock."

"Right. Ever have that with your work calendar?"

"Every week." I laugh, but it's really not funny. "It's something I've just come to accept over time. The pain of being overbooked has become a part of who I am at WL. I tell you Eve, getting my calendar cleaned up is going to be a transformation in and of itself. I can't get my head around how my day will change. I have no idea what to expect, other than a lot of backlash."

So Eve got us to my breakthrough project. It's actually a few smaller projects that fit together to make a huge impact. First, I will meet with Marilyn and educate her on my new work day, so she can help me better defend my calendar. Next, she and I will book time with my teams. I have no idea what this will look like, but Eve wants me to just try something. Nothing is written in stone, so if one approach doesn't work, I will try another. Finally, armed with my three questions, I'm going to begin walking the gembas of my team. God, I can't believe I just used a damn Japanese word in my assignment.

"Let's prepare you a little more for this one," Eve says. "What are some of the reactions you can expect when you start being present with your teams?"

I try to imagine doing this, and it's not that hard. I am going to make this happen. But it will be weird. "I think there will be mixed reactions. Some yes-men behavior. Maybe a few blank stares."

Eve nods. "Right. At first, don't expect this to be remotely comfortable or productive. All you have to do is put yourself in their shoes."

"Yes. I get that." I don't want to imagine that, because I don't want to have Lora in my head any more than she already is.

"See where it goes, Joel. Keep your mind open, so you can adapt over time. Sense and adapt."

"I think I got this."

Reflections

Attending meetings currently justifies and validates my existence.

Changing how I lead means I have to change my day.

Every hour of the day should not be booked. Leave time to reflect and learn.

Don't expect perfection when walking the gemba.

Be intentional with my visits and my questions.

Use the three, can't-fail leader questions.

New Joel

"What are you doing home?" Cele looks up from paying bills at the kitchen table.

"Hello, I'm New Joel, the one who wants to be an agile leader."

"Oh, right, New Joel." She stands up, and we meet each other halfway for a kiss. My sweet Cele is a doubter. Why would she buy in? She's been putting up with me getting run over at my job for as long as I have.

"Yeah." After proclaiming my love for her, I share with her that part of my vision to be an agile leader is to be more balanced. I'm going to try to be home by 5:30 p.m. most nights. New Joel wants to be around his family, and wants to get a break from his stressful job.

"That's great, Joel. I mean, New Joel. What about Lora and Rick? I know they sent you to coaching, but this sounds like a huge jump for them. And you."

"I've talked with them. It's going to be really challenging." So I try to manage expectations that it's not going to work out every night.

"Right, no promises." I know that sound in her voice. Cele has already dialed her expectations to zero. "You coming to Caroline's basketball game at 6:30?"

"Yep."

"Great. She'll love seeing you. You've missed a ton of games. She's really improved since the start of the season." Cele stops herself. "But what about Ironman training? How's that going to work?"

"I will figure it out as I go. With a coach and a vision, I intend to make this change permanent, Cele. New Joel wants balance...for good. He wants...all of it. And you."

"Mmm...I really like New Joel." Cele and I kiss again.

Just then, Cici bounces in the kitchen and pries us apart so she can get in the middle of her parents. We pick her up and hug her. Snuggles and giggles and family. It's the best moment of the day. Maybe the week. Golden time.

Cici holds our faces in her little hands and kisses us. Then she turns to me with five-year old concern. "Daddy, what are you doing home already? Did you get fired?"

So much for golden time.

"No, sweetheart. I came home because I live here, and love the people who live here."

Reflections

My family has let go of me in ways I don't like. I want them back.

My vision impacts everyone.

Francie Van Wirkus

Crickets

The first time I went to my teams, no one was there. They were in some team meeting that neither Marilyn nor I knew about. I was relieved and disappointed, all at once. Scared of my own teams. How telling is that? Amazing how change can completely rip away my self-confidence, to the point where I'm looking for a way out. It's a cliché, but it's true: the only way out of this is through it.

Looking back, I really wasn't ready that first time. I would have been a total dork. I'm sure they still think I am a dork, a well-dressed one, anyway, but I really had no intent worked out in my head that time. For the second round, I had better prepared myself, and was full of intention. I have my three questions with me, but I wonder if I should just forget them for these first few visits. Maybe I should just tell them what I'm doing. There's a concept. State my path, and then walk it. It's part of my vision; I should share it, right?

For my second chance, I still have no idea what I'm doing, and yet I'm pushing forward. I know I'm going to screw it up, but I can almost hear Eve's words, à la Obi-Wan Kenobi, about trusting the coaching, and not to aim for perfection. *May the force be with you.* I sure as hell hope so, because this could be an epic fail. At least I've got a good suit on my shoulders. I always feel a little more confident in a Boglioli.

I chose a work area that has a few resources whom I know fairly well. In particular, a lead resource named Karen will be a great person to start a conversation with. We worked on a project together last year. In a sea of people who just said yes to me, she was always so honest and direct. Plus, she was friendly and passionate about her work. She is definitely a great person to start with. Go with the familiar, right? And, why don't I work with her more if I like her so much? I'm so busy, I just forget.

When I arrived at the team area, there are actual people there this time. Weirdness happened immediately. I never noticed it before, but when resources saw me coming, they seemed to duck out of the way. It seems much quieter now than just 20 seconds ago, when I walked onto the floor.

Have they always done this? Hopefully this didn't have anything to do with me clearing unnecessary meetings off my calendar. Maybe I'm just paranoid.

God, I hope Karen's in her cubie. I walk up...score! She is and turns to greet me with a big smile. Whew. We start chatting about her two boys who play hockey and baseball. She lost weight, thanks to cutting out all diet soda. Who knew diet soda made you fat? Go figure. Anyway, she is a really pleasant and smart person. I want to ask more about her weight loss, but I haven't seen her in so long, it feels inappropriate. Now I miss the days when we talked more often.

Karen announces that her manager Vijay has the day off. I tell her that I'm here to see the team, not Vijay. Just to say hi.

Karen smiles and just says "Okay."

That moment registers with me loud and clear: my teams don't expect to interact with me. Crap. There is awkward silence. I can feel the heat of discomfort running up my back. She is waiting for me to be a director, and I am struggling to be a leader. It's time to just spew the truth.

"I'm going to try and be more present with my teams and managers, Karen. It's a new leader behavior I'm working on. I want to be a better leader."

"That's great, Joel." She's smiling, waiting. "Please, have a seat."

I sit in her guest chair.

"Does this have anything to do with you canceling out of project status meetings? I caught word of that."

I smile. Change is happening. It's scary and cool, all at once. "Sort of. Are you sure you have time for this? I want to respect your time."

"You're fine. I miss working with you." She pauses. Two people have walked by her cubie already. I don't look to see who they are; I try to really focus on Karen. Given the weirdness when I walked in, I'm sure the team is doing reconnaissance.

"So, I have a ton of questions to ask you about your new leader behavior, but they are really none of my business."

"I've gotten away from spending time with my teams and managers. Truth is, I've never done much of it." I shrug. "Now I'm learning some new ways to be a better leader, and it's time I begin practicing them." I can't believe the words that just came out. Did I really say them?

"Well, that's great." Karen's phone vibrates twice, but she doesn't check it. "I'm guessing that the people who don't know you as well might be freaked out about it."

"Freaked out? About just being here?" Eve is more right by the moment, and I hate it.

Karen's phone vibrates again. Could those be texts from people in the cubies surrounding us?

"Yes, freaked out. They will think you are here to check up on them, on us. Today, they would think that because Vijay is gone. Tomorrow, they would make up some other story about why you're here. Maybe you should just tell us all in a team meeting. You know, set some context about what you're doing with everyone."

"I guess I could do that. Do you know what meeting I can have 15 minutes of?"

Karen opens SharePoint to look up a meeting agenda. "I'll put you on for 30 minutes next week Monday."

"I don't need more than 15 minutes," I protest.

"Let's do 30, in case people have questions." She scans Outlook to invite me. "Ooo, it looks like you're open, too. Cool!"

"Awesome. I'll make sure to ask Marilyn." I can't believe I just agreed to this. My back is wet with sweat. I can almost hear Meryll say, *that is political suicide! You're going to be sent away!*

"Are you doing this with all of your teams?" Karen is clicking ahead of my monumental breakthrough project. She's already over the awkwardness. It's almost as if she has been waiting for this.

"Uh, yeah, I am. I guess if I do it for one team, I should for all of them."

Karen's phone vibrates again. She stuffs it in her Vera Bradley bag where its vibrations are only barely audible.

"How about I get with the other leads from your area, and have them do the same for their team meetings? If you're going to be more present with all of us, we might have some questions about it."

"That would be great, Karen. Thank you for connecting the dots for me. If you have any schedule problems, just ask Marilyn."

"Sure thing, Joel. I think what you're doing is cool. I'm excited to see where it goes for us, and for you."

"Just one more question, and then I should go." My toes are literally scrunched tight in my shoes. I'm a nervous wreck. "You seem so accepting of me doing this, and yet you think others will freak out. Why aren't *you* freaking out?"

Karen smiles. "I heard that agile is coming to WL. I'm super stoked about it. I was thinking maybe you are trying to change because we are going agile."

"Very insightful." I nod. "That's exactly what's happening. We are going agile someday, and so I'm trying to change my leadership style."

"Before I came here, I worked on a scrum team. It was really different and really good. The leaders we had struggled with it, but overall they were able to figure out how to help us."

"That's cool. I had no idea you had prior agile experience. You and I should have coffee some time, so you can tell me more about what worked and what didn't."

"Huh." Karen raised her eyebrows. "You are really serious about this."

"Yes, I am. So much that I'm willing to screw it up at your next team meeting to give it a try."

"I would love to have coffee with you. Networking, you know? I've sorta had to let go of that when I started working here. It will be cool to start thinking that way again."

"Thanks. I will set something up for us. If you have other Agilists in your midst, bring them along.'"

"Sure thing. But the first time we meet, I'm not sharing you. It's so cool to get director time. I want to keep you all to myself." Her phone vibrates again. Maybe that is another Agilist wanting to come along…

I chuckle. "Fair enough. Next week, then?"

"Yes. Looking forward to it, Joel."

I thank her, and then she has one more request. "This might sound weird, but you're probably better off not showing up in a suit and tie. Far too pretentious for our group."

I stare at her. So much for the Boglioli suit. And so much for my confidence.

"Please don't be angry. It's just that, well, if you want to spend time with us, it might help. Right now, you're just one of 'The Suits'."

"Uh, I'm not mad at you." I'm stunned! "Thank you for your advice, Karen. I will definitely reflect on it."

"Great."

What just happened? I feel the need to call Eve, but I'm not sure what I'd tell her. *Hello, I just walked my team's gemba and I'm sweaty and happy and scared.* No way. This is a moment to share with Jack and Meryll.

"Let me get this straight," Meryll looks at me blankly, "You're going to your team's meetings to tell them that you're going to be more present in their areas?"

"Basically, yeah."

"They are going to pepper you with questions. You'll be stuck in there for an hour," Meryll predicts. She's looking especially tired today.

"That might not be a bad thing," Jack offers. "Besides, it's going to be a lot more fun hanging with the teams than it is being a prisoner in endless meetings."

Meryll points her manicured finger at Jack. "That's what I'm talking about, Joel. Are you just appeasing feedback that people gave you? They don't understand how busy you are. So now you're going to just be *hanging with the teams*." She imitates Jack. "What exactly is that? Gonna start writing some code? And, why is that better than being on a project status conference call?"

"Joel, she sounds pissed. I think it's because you beat her to this assignment."

"Shut up." She rolls her eyes.

Jack pretends to take a punch. What did I ever do before he worked with us? I put up with Meryll's drama, that's what. Not only is Jack smart and young, he knows how to neutralize her crap.

I tell them the final part of my adventure, that Karen requested I didn't wear a suit. Otherwise, I will remain one of *The Suits*, and unreachable.

This sends Meryll over the edge. "That's ridiculous." She throws up her arms. "They can't tell you how to dress."

"Think of all the dry cleaning money you'll save, Joel," Jack offers in jest. I think.

"The problem is, I have no idea what to wear. I own a few pairs of khaki pants. We aren't allowed to wear jeans, so…"

"Listen to you, *I have no idea what to wear!* Good grief." She is really wound up. We spar quite a bit with the way we interact, so I'm not bothered by her words. Over the years, we have disagreed on some big things, and always found a way to work it out. I'm sure this will be the same way, eventually.

"Just curious." I ask. "Have you met with your coach at all, Meryll?" This makes Jack laugh.

"Yes." She grimaces.

"I will take you shopping." Jack announces. "After all, I was the one hired away from the hip-happenin' company, where we got to wear cool stuff all of the time."

"Wait, you have clothes like that? Business casual?"

"Yes, Joel. And, I'm serious about taking you shopping. We'll be shopping bros."

As awkward as that sounds, I could really use the help from someone who's shopped for those clothes. I accept his offer and we plan on going to his favorite stores over the weekend.

"What are you going to do, shop during one of the color coded times on your calendar?" Meryll sneers.

"We're going on the weekend, *moron*." Jack relishes his payback.

I can't resist beating on Meryll. "Laugh all you want at my color coded calendar, Meryll. I was home by 5:30 the last two days. That hasn't happened in…well, forever. Cele nearly fell over. I saw my kid's basketball game. It was the best." I breathe faster, because just the thought of the last two nights has me excited. There is hope to have more balance. "Now that I have a taste of what balance can be like, I'm hooked."

"Very cool," Jack admires.

I'm still hung up on the fact that Jack doesn't wear the clothes at WL that he wore at his last job. "So, I'm trying to remember your first day, Jack. Did you wear a suit or your old clothes?"

"I was told in my interviews that it's expected that I wear a suit. That all leaders in our area wear them." Jack seems embarrassed about it now. "I guess I was too excited about working for WL to care at the time."

"Whatever. We're professionals, and we wear suits," Meryll proclaims. "Lora is not going to like this."

"Huh." I look at Jack's suit. "I just assumed you had them at your last job. I never would have guessed that you were instructed on how to dress. I'm sure Lora was behind it."

"This is going too far, Joel." Meryll is pacing in my office, again. I tried to imagine what she might look like in something other than a suit jacket. All I come up with is a straitjacket, and that's not a pretty picture for my teammate. I squint as if I can physically squeeze out the image that I created.

"First, you don't have to listen to this lead. What does she know anyway?" More pacing. The floor shakes a little under her stomping, as if she weighs 300 pounds, but she's not even close to that. Because of the stomping, her black heels now look overdone. And they are too high. Just like the ones most of the other women at WL wear with their suits. That crisp skirt she has on probably cost $300... "She has overstepped her boundary. You are in this vulnerable state because of all that feedback you asked for. Now they are just going to run you over."

"Please leave Karen out of this. She offered me advice. It was a very neutral conversation," I say.

"Unlike this one," Jack snorts. He probably wishes he was still at his hip-happenin' company, wearing his upscale, casual men's wear, far away from Lora and Meryll.

"Look, I care about you, Joel." Meryll's voice softens, and she stops pacing. "I don't like to see you in such a vulnerable position. You're a strong, successful leader. I want it to stay that way."

"I can't stay the same, Meryll. I need to get better. If I'm going to get better, I have to be a little vulnerable."

"What is better?"

I tell Meryll what she already knows: that I don't have all the answers, but I'm trusting my agile coach to help get me to a new place as a leader. I tell her how none of it feels right, and in fact, it feels really wrong.

"Because it is! I'm worried, Joel."

"Don't be," I assure her. "I will be fine."

"You are opening Pandora's Box." She warns, almost pleads.

"I'm so miserable right now, that I'm willing to open the box to find out if it can be better."

Reflections

I am not as good of a leader as I thought.

Going to Karen's desk was hard.

Karen's advice for me was a gift.

The snappy dresser comment on my feedback was actually sarcasm.

My teams don't take me seriously.

I think I'm too far away from my teams for them to take me seriously.

What does it mean to take me seriously anyway?

Meryll sees vulnerability as weakness. I don't think they are the same.

I loved getting home by 5:30 two days in a row!

Shopping Bros

Since I was home at 5:25 p.m., Cele and I had a chance to talk alone before heading to Eric's hockey game. A perfect chance to remind her of my vision to become an agile leader, and to tell her about my *go & see* project. I knew she'd love the part about my calendar almost as much as I do. I try to set the expectation that I don't know what I'm doing, that I'll mess it up, but in the long run, this will be a good thing. She's all for it. Then I tell her I'm going shopping with Jack this weekend to build on my new leadership style.

"You're going clothes shopping for work with *who*?" Cele asks.

"Jack. You know, new guy." I try to make it sound like I do this all of the time even though Cele knows better. "We're bro shopping for my new clothes."

"Bro shopping." She says flatly. "Is this one of Eve's bright ideas?"

"No it's Jack's. Well, actually…" I give Cele the background about *go & see* (not the lean part) and how my conversation with Karen has caused me to rethink my wardrobe.

"Huh," She says. "New Joel goes shopping with New Guy. Next will be girlfriends and a red sports car in the driveway?"

I assure Cele that it's just clothes, not a mid-life crisis. No girlfriends, although a red sports car would be nice. I just want to be more approachable. And Eve doesn't even know that I'm doing it. I remind her that I can't be left to make fashion choices on my own. She's in full agreement on that. And that younger, hipper Jack is just the guy to help. In the end, Cele likes my idea and says she fully supports it because I look "cuter" when I'm not in a suit. All these things I am learning about how I look. I can't wait to go bro shopping.

Francie Van Wirkus

Reflections

Changing what I wear at work is a bigger deal than I expected.

Dress Rehearsal

I couldn't wait for my next meeting with Eve. Not only was I anxious to share with her how my breakthrough project went, it was my first day of upscale business casual. I can't tell you how good it feels to not be in a tie. I'm warm, comfortable, and surprisingly confident. Hopefully, I won't spill coffee on myself and ruin my new clothes. It reminds me of the first day of grade school, when I didn't want to get my new athletic shoes dirty. I can almost hear my mother, "Joel, try to keep your tennies clean." As if a 10-year old boy had that capability.

That morning I didn't swim early, so I am home while my family is up and getting ready for the day. I'm in the kitchen packing a few snacks when 15-year old Caroline walks in.

"Who are you supposed to be?"

"Uh, your Dad?" Just pretend nothing is different. Man, bro shopping is already causing a stir.

"You're wearing, like, young people clothes," She accuses.

Just then Eliott and Erik walk in. "Who's wearing young people clothes?" Eliott asks.

Erik whistles. "Wow Dad. Look at you!"

"Are you gonna be on TV or something?" Eliott asks.

"Who's gonna be on TV?" Five year old Cici walks into the kitchen. "I wanna be on TV too!"

"No one's going to be on TV." Caroline practically scolds her family.

Cici hugs me. "You smell good. You smell like new clothes!"

Now the four children are picking apart my outfit, and making all manner of sound effects. I felt so good, and now I feel…dissected. Caroline is touching the fabric of my shirt. So worried about people's reactions at work, I completely underestimated my family's reaction.

"Does Mom know about this?" Eliott asks. Seven year-olds are all about the rules.

"Yes." I own my look. It's just another morning, just another day.

"Seriously Dad." Caroline stands in front of me. "What are you doing?"

I tell them some of the back story of being more approachable. It resonates with the older two, but the younger ones were no longer interested when I said I wasn't going to be on TV.

My snack is packed so I fly out the door. They are still talking about me. *Go & see* is quite the disruption. Yet the scene in my kitchen was only the beginning.

When I arrive at work, Marilyn is on me. "What's up with you?" Her experienced eyes scrutinize my new clothes. Man, I hadn't given any thought to this. I'm a guy; can't I just wear my clothes and live my life?

"Just part of New Joel. I'm changing how I lead." I shrug. *Nothing new to see here. Keep believing it.*

"Did Cele buy those for you?" More accusation.

"No. I did." I don't have to tell her about Jack. She will never get bro shopping. Rumors will fly.

"Huh." She folds her arms, and looks at me with doubt. The same kind Cele had.

"No sports cars, no girlfriends, no mid-life crisis. Just more casual, stylish clothes."

"Huh."

At least today I have an escape. "Well, I've gotta run and meet Eve."

Eve notices my clothes right away. Her green eyes flicked over me with approval. The kind that passes inspection, not the kind that gets you dates. Not that I want a date with her. Never mind.

"Are all of your suits at the dry cleaners?"

"No." I smile. I tell Eve the story of my *go & see* adventure to Karen's desk, the meetings we planned so I can tell them why I'm going to be more visible, and of course, her advice on ditching the suit.

"So, this is not a temporary thing? Not just for these meetings?" Eve asks.

"Right. I'm going to try and dress differently from now on."

"Did Cele buy them for you?"

"No. Jack and I went shopping. He called it Bro Shopping."

"Dorks."

"Maybe so, but do I look like one now?" I smooth my hands over my shirt and puff out my chest.

"No." Eve smiles. "What did Cele say?"

"She freaked a little, even after I explained it all to her. But secretly, I think she was thrilled to be relieved of the task of dressing me." I can't tell her the part about how Cele thinks I look cuter this way.

"Nice. A woman's got to seriously wonder when her man has a sudden change of wardrobe. I just want to make sure you are bringing her along for the ride."

I never thought of it that way, but she's right. "Good point, again."

"I have to say, you look *better* this way."

She wants to say *cuter*, I just know it!

We review my reflections together. I'm amazed at how many reflections I have, just from setting up plans for spending time with my teams. I haven't actually done it yet. I had one visit to Karen, and it sent a large amount of change in motion.

"First, how about that getting home at 5:30 p.m. business?" She gives me a high five.

I tell her it was definitely the highlight of all the things that happened over the week. It felt so good to steal just an extra 30 minutes to talk with Cele. That wouldn't have happened if I had arrived home at 6:30 p.m. I'm excited about the possibilities of a better calendar. I will be able to see more of my kids' events and games, and be more of a contributor in the family. I don't like being the one no one can depend on. But with all this upside, I don't know if it's really going to work. It almost seems too good to be true.

She chides me about being hesitant to try my new calendar. I assure that as good as it felt to change my calendar and be home earlier, I am not out of the woods yet. There is no way Lora was actually listening in our meeting. She is going to be confused about it someday soon, so I need to make sure I'm ready. But I can't be ready for all of it. There will be aftershocks of this calendar thing beyond what I can imagine. I can't worry about them, but I can expect them.

She asks me more questions about my discussion with Karen. She's encouraged that I found an Agilist so close to me.

"The feedback Karen gave you is a huge gift," Eve beams.

"Yes, I know. I never thought one of my first steps would include taking advice from one of my resources." I tell Eve that Karen has agile experience, and we plan to talk together so I can learn from her.

"Excellent." Eve commends me, but then her face changes. She has that look on her face, the one where I'm about to get yelled at. Man, what did I do now?

"Oh, and I didn't tell you the wildest part of that visit." I sit up straight in my chair. I tell her how people scattered when I arrived on the floor, and how quiet it got within five minutes of me being there. The worse part was when Karen's phone kept vibrating. Of course her teammates were messing with her.

"How did you feel?" Eve was smiling.

"Like I didn't belong there, for sure." It's hard to tell her any of this. "I also felt like I was…a game. I'm so out of reach, that when I show up, people can't handle themselves."

"Great observations. You went there with the right intention, or you might not have noticed as much as you did."

I chuckle. "You're trying to make me feel better. It's not working."

"I'm not. One of the key things about *go & see* is intention. We are just beginning our work on this, but you are already off to a great start." Eve sips her matcha latte. "What you experienced is really challenging, Joel. Your inner caveman is uncomfortable with all this change. Even when it's good."

Yeah, all of this from just one *go & see* exercise. "I'm glad I got the first one out of the way. It's incredible how much I learned without even asking the three questions."

"Right, you are just easing into this. Safe to say, now you know why we are easing into this."

"Yes. I don't think I could have handled any more."

Eve assures me that I did great, even if it doesn't feel that way. Then she tells me there is more easing in to do before I can ask *go & see* questions. More to fix. How does she see it all? It's like she has a playbook and she's just marching us down the field.

"Joel, I've been waiting for the right moment to coach you on this. We've got so much to cover, that I have held off. I realize now there will never be a good time, so I'm just going to lay it on you. You have to get to the next level, and this assignment is a big part of it."

"Lay it on me." I pretend to be happy and excited.

She takes a breath. "Stop calling people *resources*."

"I didn't call Karen a resource to her face," I protest. Why did I defend? I can't help it.

"Of course not. But good agile leaders do not call their people resources."

There is a pause while Eve lets her request sink in. I imagine Meryll sitting here listening to this request, and rolling her eyes. I have to get that drama queen out of my head. Focus…

"Can I call them…teams?"

"Yes," Eve assures me. "Call them people, talent, teams, or what they care about: developers, designers, or testers. Just never, ever resources."

Great, another thing I'm bad at. But I don't think it's just me. "Does that mean we have to change the title of the Human Resources department to the Human People department?"

"I get it," Eve assures me. "Most of us have been guilty of this. In the world of projects-based work, you need people with specific skills such as a developer with expertise in a platform. We've all let it slide into how we speak. HR is a prime example."

"Can a word really change anything? Especially when everyone else is doing it?"

"Once again, it's culture, Joel. It began to be misused when there was too much focus on trying to build projects around skills, and then we forgot that these people with the skills have other differences about them, like their capabilities and personalities. Pressures, time constraints…it was just easier to treat people as replaceable, even interchangeable."

I hold my head in my hands. "This isn't even an agile thing, is it?" I don't look up.

"No, but it fits right in with the idea of people and interactions over processes and tools. And respect for people, which is a key concept in lean leadership. We'll get to all of that someday. Right now, this is a basic respect thing."

"It's so ingrained in our culture, I don't know if anyone will notice that I'm not saying it."

"Your teams will."

"Huh. It's for them…" I start remembering scenes, even from this week, of Jack, Meryll, Lora and I using the word *resources* wrong.

"You can ask Karen if you don't believe me."

"I was just thinking that." I smile. "Not that I don't believe you. I just…first it was the feedback and now this resources business. My reality is not really the current reality," I sigh. "It's depressing."

Eve's eyes soften with sympathy. "If life were perfect, I wouldn't be here."

"Yeah, but it feels like I'm just messing up all over the place."

Eve shifts in her seat. "I'm not sure how far we'll progress together, Joel. You are quickly learning this part of change requires going to some dark places. It's part of the journey."

"You sound like one of those unreachable, but cool-sounding social media posters," I laugh.

"For sure. But in this case, it has substance. You will live it."

I ask Eve about my inner caveman. I want to do this, but how am I going to curb the urge to use the word? How am I going to keep from falling back into my old calendar? Eve tells me I walked right into my next breakthrough project: to not use the word *resources* in place of people, ever again. I'm to tell Jack, Meryll, and Karen about my project. Then I'm going to ask them to call it out whenever they hear me say the word.

"I want you to ask Lora and Rick to help you too. But let's begin with these three people. They are in your corner, which is a safer place to begin."

"I'm not sure Meryll is in my corner," I protest.

"Well, who do you trust more, Meryll or Lora?"

She's always got a good point. "Meryll is really wound up with the stuff I'm doing. I thought she was getting agile coaching. Shouldn't she be a little more open to my challenges?"

"She is getting coaching, but I'm not privy to any of her journey. It's pretty obvious she's in a different place on her journey, and she's scared."

"I'm the one sticking my neck out to change. So far, she's hasn't done a thing."

"Right. The changes you are making scare her. She is scared for you and for herself."

"I get that. I'm vulnerable and uncomfortable, and she knows this is her future."

"It is if she wants to be an agile leader."

Reflections

My challenges scare me, and they scare others.

My vision scares me and excites me.

I have not been respecting my teams.

I want to change.

I am less afraid of change than my peers.

I love my notebook!

Test Drive

Never before have I been nervous to join my team for one of their meetings, but this *go & see* work has me wound up. I'm headed to the first of five team meetings, to share my plan to be a more present leader. The meetings don't all happen on the same day, but they are all the same week. Good thing I have a newly organized calendar to accommodate for the visits.

The first meeting was with Karen's team. The project manager kicked off the team meeting in a dreary manner, and then it was my turn to speak. It seems like these team meetings haven't improved since I started here. They are probably just as demotivating to teams as they were then. Why can't it be better? Will agile change any of this? Could I change any of this?

I share what I'm doing with the team and their manager, at a very high level. I'm getting coached to be a better leader, and one of the things I am going to begin doing is to *go and see* my managers, my teams, our work, our processes. I assure the team that I'm practicing every day, and that I will likely screw something up. Please cut me some slack. I also assure them that I'm not doing this to check up on people or control things. I am doing it to have a better view of what I can do to help them.

I share with them the questions I'm going to be coached to ask. Everyone dutifully writes them down or types them on their device. At least there were no texts flying back and forth while I was there.

"What if we don't know the answer to these questions?" A team member asked.

"This will be new to all of us, so don't worry about having the right answer. There is a big learning curve with this for me and for all of you. Let's just try it and roll with it."

"Joel, is this part of bringing agile into WL?" Karen asks.

"Yes, and it's about building a work place that continuously improves. I'm also getting coached on how to be a lean leader."

"As in Toyota lean?" Karen asks.

"Yes. Only for us it's about knowledge work so it's different." I'm not sharing any secrets, but it feels really weird to be this honest with them.

"So we're going to use lean?"

Crap.

"The person who is coaching me believes that I need to learn lean leader standard work in order to be a better leader. Honestly, I had no idea I'd be learning about lean leader standard work, but I am. It's not clear where it's all going, but I'm trusting my coach and rolling with it."

"So we're not using lean." Karen presses me.

I smile at her effort to gain clarity. "I'm not saying either way about lean. I'm only being taught some concepts of lean. I'm being coached by them so that I can become a better leader."

My manager Vijay looks slightly uncomfortable. "Joel, what do you see as the manager's role in all of this?"

Ah, I've worried Vijay by invading his territory. Or maybe he's worried that Lora is going to try this on him. Or both. "Great question, Vijay. Everyone in this room has an important part of how we get our work done. Since I'm just learning about how this technique works, I don't have an answer for you right now."

I ask Vijay and the team to give me a chance to practice, and then maybe Vijay can shadow me to learn more. What did I just say? Ugh, I felt like I went off the reservation offering that to Vijay. But it also felt right. I have to check with Eve after this meeting. She did tell me I could call her any time…

I left that first meeting sweaty and happy that I accomplished my task. I felt like I really put myself out there. Though I am not quite sure what *out there* means.

Thankfully, Eve took my call. "You're right, we haven't covered everything about *go & see*. But from what you know already, and what you know about your reporting structures, do you think your managers should be doing this?"

"I think I just asked you the same question, Eve."

"So what do you think? Apply what you've learned so far."

"Managers are a part of *go & see*," I guess. "I don't see any reason why directors would be the only ones doing it. Wouldn't we all be smarter about what's going on if we all saw what was going on?"

"That's right. You're getting the concept, Joel. We can talk more about it next time, but I am very happy you called me about it. Just be sure Vijay doesn't feel like you are taking something away from him."

"I'm pretty sure he feels that way even though I assured him I'm just practicing. Maybe I'm overthinking all of it."

"No more thinking about it. You know what to do for the other four meetings."

She's right, again. Armed with renewed confidence in being inexperienced, I follow through with the other four meetings. The same darn question about lean came up in each of these meetings. It was pretty clear to me that Vijay's team had talked with the other teams ahead of me. Sort of the meeting before the meeting had occurred. Overall, I felt like I accomplished what I set out to do: share with everyone my vision to become a better leader and how I'll begin practicing *go & see* with them.

Reflections

Lean is a dirty word at WL.

Karen and Vijay are change champions and my allies.

Francie Van Wirkus

Positive Thinking

I cleared things up with Vijay, and he is now very excited to begin practicing what I'm practicing. I asked him to please hold off until I get better at it. I tell him I am looking forward to the day when he shadows me and we do it together. Vijay's face lit up and I thought he might jump out of his skin. He asked if he could research the topic in the meantime. I was careful on how to answer this question.

I realize how someone of my position can say something is an idea and it suddenly turns into a full blown assignment. I'm very clear with Vijay that I'm not assigning him to do anything, but I am encouraging him to research the topic and see how it might apply to him and his peers.

"Would you like a report on it?" Vijay asked.

I don't know why, but that didn't seem like something Eve would ask me to do, so I told Vijay no. This woman is really getting in my head. Maybe that is the whole idea. When I'm out for sushi, trying to decide between the firefly specialty roll and the spicy tuna special, am I going to wonder *what would Eve do*?

"Let's talk about it together instead. We can probably learn from each other better that way. Maybe that can be the way we begin you shadowing me? You know, we talk about what you think *go & see* means to you and your peers, and then we practice." Vijay looks surprised and then nods in happy agreement.

That conversation felt good and weird and exciting, all at once. I have no idea what I'm doing other than the fact that I made Vijay very happy.

I was a little nervous before I met Karen for coffee. A lot nervous, actually. I thought of what was uncomfortable about it. The bottom line is that I didn't want to screw things up. I'm not sure what I would screw up. Given what I've shared with you already, things are in fact, pretty screwed up already. Still, I could make it worse. So it was a real anxiety. It's ridiculous but real. And directors don't meet with people like this unless they are interviewing them for a new project assignment. Eve's assignment was pushing me into difficult territory. And pushing me to see that I am indeed afraid of my own team.

I found courage by thinking positive thoughts about the kind of leader I want to be. I want to know my teams better. I want to be someone people can trust. I want respect, not cell phone texts behind my back. I don't know all the ways to do this, but meeting with Karen is a good first step. I got this.

Did Karen have to work up to our meeting like I did? She seemed to be excited about sharing her experience with me, so hopefully she's not dreading it. Maybe she thought I was going to ask her about a new opportunity. No, I was clear that I wanted to hear about agile. Listen to me, I'm floundering.

"Karen, can I ask your honest opinion?"

"Sure." She looks confident but her voice sounds a little reluctant.

"What do you think of the way people...well, leaders use the word *resources*?"

Karen shrugs. "It's not the best. But mostly it doesn't bother me."

"You're holding back, aren't you?" I smile. What am I doing? I'm not breaking any rules, but it feels so...*wrong*. "Tell me what you're *really* thinking, Karen."

A crooked smile crosses her face.

"Please don't hold back."

"How do I know you won't tell someone else about our conversation?"

"I promise I won't judge, report, or share your responses. Unless of course you want to hurt someone or break the law. Then, I might have to tell someone."

"Fair enough."

I offer to pinky swear to confirm it, but she didn't think it was necessary.

"You sure you're ready to hear this? I realize you're working on being a better leader and all that, but this one is tough."

I look directly at her, "Lay it on me."

"Calling people *resources* instead of people is the worst *ever*. It's dehumanizing and insulting." She stops for a moment.

"Go on." I encourage her.

"It's even in the title of a large department here, *human resources*. Ugh. What I don't understand is how no one in this company seems to notice it's happening, or care about it. It's really depressing."

"Thank you for being honest with me, Karen." I sound like Eve. She is completely taking over my psyche. Gah!

"You're welcome. I really don't want you to think I'm a complainer."

"I don't. I asked you, remember?"

"Yes, but that doesn't mean much at WL. We say we want the truth, but then when it's revealed, things have a way of changing. Usually not for the better."

"We've all gotten burned here by that one. I'm sorry that has happened in the past, Karen. I'm working hard to change how I lead. You probably won't notice much at first, but over time, I hope the new leader in me is a positive change."

Karen laughs and tells me she's noticed plenty in me already. "You're not wearing a tie, for Heaven's sake! And you've talked to the teams. It's like, huge." Karen's face gets serious again. "I believe you are making permanent change, but don't be surprised if people think you're just doing it until you get bored. Or, until WL introduces the next shiny tool. Remember that Winning Together push? That kind of thing."

"Yes I do. They are not good memories."

I don't share with Karen that I will never forget Winning Together. I lived that employee engagement program for eight months, with Lora on my back the entire time. The program was the spawn of an employee survey. If that sounds negative, it's supposed to. After the meetings and action plans for the employee survey, someone got the idea of making a new and improved employee engagement program. Winning Together was born.

Lora wanted to have the best employee survey results. The managers had this one handled. Employee engagement and recognition programs usually fall into their realm. But since Lora always wants to be first, she turned to micromanagement and drove us all nuts. She was on a mission to have the best reports, meetings, and stories about how people loved the new program. The managers had this one handled.

Thankfully, it died the same year. All those meetings, fluffy status reports, outcome reports…so much time and talking. All we have to show for it now is employee survey numbers that are slightly higher, which might be within the variance, and a gift card program for a popular coffee house.

"Thanks for noticing my changes. Please promise me that if you ever hear me say the word *resources* when I mean people or teams, you will call me on it."

"I'd be happy to. But," she holds up a hand, "If I feel like I'm in a situation where I might get fired, I'm not going to call you on it. I need my job, Joel. Mortgage, kids…"

"Yes. Thank you."

I spend the next 30 minutes hearing about Karen's agile experience at her former employer. She had worked as a scrum master, and on a support team that sat with a scrum team. She loved her experience, and had only good things to say about agile. In fact, it was pretty clear she loved agile and couldn't wait to work that way again. It was great to hear what she learned there. I didn't understand half of what she said about scrum, so I asked her for some good books to read or videos (can't I just YouTube agile?). Just another thing I need to study to get myself to the next level. How many levels are there anyway?

"When are we going to adopt agile? I heard it's in our strategy, but I haven't heard anything since."

I tell her it's coming to WL this year, but I'm not sure when, how big it will be, or any other detail about it. I ask her if she wants to be involved, without knowing what that really means. No promises, no job, no guarantees. She gives me an emphatic "Yes!"

"You should go to training, Joel. You can read all the books you like, but it's nothing like learning it in training." Karen is adamant. "You won't regret any of it."

"Where do you go for that?"

Karen lists a few local firms, including her favorite one because everyone she worked with raved about the training class and the follow-up coaching. The classes are five days long. That seemed like a very long time to learn something called agile. But then, Karen assured me that you need five days to really immerse yourself in it. She said there is a two-day class for leaders, but that if I really want to connect with my people, I should go to a five-day class. I tell Karen I will ask my coach about it, to find out when would be a good time to go. She liked that I was going to follow through on her advice. I liked getting her advice.

Reflections

The words I (we) use - resources- is hurting the culture at WL.

No one liked Winning Together.

Karen is an agile champion.

Forbidden

Rick and I are having a one-on-one meeting in his office. As usual, we are down in the weeds about what I'm doing. He asks me about coaching, and I give him a high-level answer about it being challenging and uncomfortable, and also I'm making progress.

"I heard that you told your teams that we are going to use lean at WL," Rick sighs. "I have to say, I'm disappointed that you had that discussion."

Now to answer without sounding defensive. What would Eve do? Clarify and repeat back what my purpose was, that's what. Actually, I'm pretty sure she would never be in this position in this meeting.

"To clarify, Rick, I did not tell the teams that we are going to use lean at WL. I told them I am being coached to be a better leader. My coach believes that using lean leader concepts will help me become a better leader."

"Huh." He always says he trusts us, but clearly he thinks I'm a dolt. "That is not the impression one of your managers had."

"Which manager? I can circle back with them and clarify."

Rick waves his hand. "Not necessary. I have taken care of it."

Wow. Wonder what's behind all of that? No, I can't care about it. Not my focus.

"Joel, another thing about lean that I think you should know." Rick leans back in his executive chair. All that's missing is a smoking robe and pipe. Maybe a glass of cognac and a mustache. "Okay, so you're getting coached on lean concepts. I appreciate how you are sharing with your teams what you're doing, but you need to change your words." Rick leans forward. "Avoid saying the word lean. It's bad for our transformation plans. When people think of lean, they think of Toyota and layoffs. The last thing we need here is a rumor about layoffs."

This is nuts, but I need to know more. I can't resist. "So, if it's not lean, what is it?"

"Call it whatever you like, Joel." Rick waves his hand again. Must be the new VP move of the day. "Just avoid using lean. I don't want our resources getting upset over nothing. It could really spin up into a negative thing, and if the press gets a hold of us having layoffs, we'll really be in deep. Things are so competitive right now, we can't afford a misstep. Neither you nor I have time for that kind of back pedaling."

"If we don't know if we are using lean, I don't know why I would avoid using the word."

"The topic shouldn't even be up for discussion because we like to keep things calm, not uncertain. Why open up a can of worms if we don't have to?"

"Rick, I respect your wishes, but can you help me understand why talking about a methodology that we may or may not use is bad for WL employees? It sounds like there is more to the story."

"There isn't." Rick said it with such certainty that there most definitely was more to the story. We must be bringing in lean. They are still talking about what it all means and they are freaked out about it. That's my guess. I would probably freak out about it too, but not enough to hide it from employees. That plan always backfires.

"Joel, I like that you are challenging me, so don't worry about your pushback. I stand firm on that decision though, so don't expect me to change my mind. I've been talking with our corporate communications folks and they are all over it. We have a dialogue going about what the word lean means to people and how WL wants to position itself with it."

"Sounds like it's already an issue."

"No, we are just having precautionary conversations."

Like he's talking about a security breach...

"Joel, if we get a jump on this now, we can avoid unnecessary noise. Think through it," he offers. "I know that once you do, you will see where we're coming from on this one."

I'm stunned for a moment. "Understood," is all I can say.

"I'm not sure you do, Joel." Rick is thoroughly enjoying his all-knowing leader of the universe position right now. "It's really critical that we clear a path that will allow us to lay the right foundation for agile. Spreading rumors about lean isn't going to help. We need our managers and resources to be focused on the job at hand, not speculation or rumors."

"Go it." I'm done. But our meeting has just begun. I have to pull out of this fast, or I will be micromanaged to some other imaginary behavioral problem. "Thank you for the context, Rick. It's very helpful."

Later, I leave Rick's office feeling heavy and annoyed. That's nothing new, but the topic is. God. He's been talking with corporate communications about it? There has to be more to the story. Even if there weren't more to the story, it's classic mishandling at the corporate level. What the hell does corporate communications know about lean anyway? Any time I've had to work with them, it takes three months to figure out what it is we are talking about. Wait, this isn't about *knowing about* lean, is it?

I mentally step back and look at this from an even higher level. Ah, I see it now. Corporate communications doesn't have to be an expert in lean to help Rick. They are experts in words and protecting decisions, which is why I've never liked or trusted that department. The majority of their existence is for corporate screens and blocks. They are the ones to call when you have a pile of crap, and you don't want people to notice it. They teach you how to hide things from employees, and how to manipulate words. In some weird way, that's the sweet spot of what's happening here, so of course they are involved with Rick.

"You can't walk around saying things like that, Joel!" Lora leans across her desk toward me. "Crap, what is this coach teaching you anyway?" She rolls her eyes. Man, she is really wound up. Maybe too much caffeine? Whatever the situation, it's too late now. I'm in the middle of Tropical Storm Lora.

"Lora, Rick and I discussed it. I'm not sure why I'm discussing it again with you." This is so classic, to rehash my mistake with two leaders. They both have to nail me for it so they can stamp their authority on me, and justify their existence.

I will never have her trust and she thinks I'm a dolt, too. "Because I wasn't there, *Jo-el.*" She stretches out saying my name, like a bossy girl I knew in sixth grade.

"Would you like for me to tell you what Rick and I discussed?" I have to play as dumb as she thinks I am, or I will look defensive. Then I'll have an action plan for the next six months to pull out of it. Nope. Not happening this time.

"Please," She huffs. I can see her trying to hold back on me. It's a miserable attempt.

I tell her about my exchange with Rick. Not the part when he made me feel like an idiot, but the context of things. And Rick's request that I not use the word lean, and the corporate communications part.

"Oh that's right. He did involve them." Lora has a distant look on her face, but before I can get a word in, she snaps out of it. "We've been talking with corporate communications to make sure we get the words right."

"That's what I hear." I'm trying so very hard to not get up and walk out. To the bar. For a long run. Anything but this room, this job.

"Joel, the change we're going to make is a really big deal." Lora was all-knowing. I was the reckless dolt who needed a good talking to. "We have to make sure we do it right, so we're not spending our energy backpedaling. We need to keep our focus on forward progress. Spreading rumors about lean isn't going to do us any favors."

"I thought I just explained what happened, Lora. I wasn't starting rumors; I was being honest with the team about my coaching."

"Well, you should know better than to be so open with the teams. Resources will freak out with that kind of information. You have to balance things, Joel. *Balance.* Being truthful is great, but not at the expense of team morale." Yes, Lora believes she is honestly helping me. Her pearls of leadership wisdom are to be cherished and practiced. I should be thanking her over and over for her generosity.

"Thank you, Lora. Rick told me the same. I see where you're coming from. I'll change my approach." I assured Lora I would no longer use the word lean, and that I would be more cognizant of my teams. Lora seemed satisfied with my *mea culpa.*

"Good. I knew you would understand it better when I explained it to you." Lora is happy again. So am I, because we're almost finished for now. "Sometimes Rick can be too vague with what he wants from us. I want to get right to the heart of things, so we can move on." Lora smiles. "You're doing good work, Joel."

"Thanks, Lora. I appreciate your help." She got to win, and I got to be the idiot.

Reflections

More roadblocks remind me how hard it is to live out my vision to change.

There is fear about using lean.

I know how it feels to be under command and control leadership - miserable.

Speculation 101

"There has to be more to the story," Meryll says as she paces the floor of my office.

"Meryll, can't you just sit down and drink your flat brown frappa-Italiano?" Jack can't resist an easy target like Meryll.

"Shut up, Jack. I can pace if I want to. Besides," she looks at the fitness tracker on her wrist, "I'm getting my steps in. And, it's a single shot coconut milk mocha."

Jack feigns astonishment. "No way."

Meryll wants to laugh at his acting, but she can't let down her guard. She'd rather he think she's mad at him than give him the satisfaction of laughing at his jokes. It's like a brother and sister type of psychological warfare, and harmless overall.

"I get tired of telling you two to shut up," I sigh. "This was about me, remember? Say, Jack. How was your four-day weekend?"

Jack grins. "Skiing, skiing, and more skiing. I loved it. My calendar is still a color-coded mess, but I'm making progress. It felt so good to get away. I'm sure you missed me tons."

"Oh for sure," Meryll sighs.

"Nice work. I love it."

"Back to Joel and the secrets of lean," Jack says.

Meryll huffs, "I just hate how Lora is so good at making us feel dumb. I can't stand it."

"Rick's no better," I say. "His language is more subtle."

"I don't like how we don't know about this lean thing." Meryll is waxing to some bigger concept. "Any time corporate communications is involved, it means someone screwed up, or they are really worried about screwing it up. This sounds like the latter, but who knows?"

"I'd rather not speculate," I say. "I want us to focus on what this means to our coaching and our breakthrough projects.

"It means that you're going to be out there on your own, that's what," Meryll sighs. "This is exactly what I was afraid would happen, Joel. You get coached and encouraged to take some huge steps. You set out to take those steps, and then you get smacked down, just like that!" She slaps her hands together. "They say they want us to get coaching, but I'm not sure they mean it. We are the ones to pay the price when they decide that coaching was a mistake."

"At least we'll have corporate communications to spin up the story nicely," Jack offers. "We don't want people to see the bodies."

Meryll sighs. "Jack, for once can you stop cracking jokes? This is serious."

"It sure is." Jack agrees. "Meryll, I take my job very seriously. Things are not at all the way I expected them to be when I started here. In fact, I don't see anything good happening at WL these days, so it's either laugh or cry. I ain't cryin'."

"That is lame, Jack," Meryll judges. "You can't change anything by laughing about it."

"Just like you can't change anything by ranting about it," Jack sneers.

"All right you two." I raise my hands. "Truce, before you kill me with your arguing."

Meryll ignores my request. Jack smirks at me, with his *what are you gonna do with us?* look. "Joel, this whole coaching scene is creeping me out. What is the point of us getting coached if we are just going to be fed to the lions?"

"Who are the lions, Rick and Lora?" Jack asks. "Or the entire company? It feels like it's more than just those two and their lean-a-phobia."

I agree with Jack. Of course it's more than just Lora and Rick. There is an entire culture working against our coaching. We can't change the culture, but we can change small things a little at a time.

"But they're not small. Look what happened to you, Joel," Meryll frets. "I am still scared about when Lora realizes just how much you have changed your day and your calendar. You know, I was going to start working on changing my calendar. Little changes, because I'm not as brave as you. Now I'm not sure I'm going to do it at all. I'm convinced she had no idea what she was agreeing to in Rick's office that day. When she does, you're going to get squashed." She takes a breath. "I don't want you to get squashed. I don't want bad things to happen to you, or any of us."

Jack rolls his eyes. "Too late for that." What a response from the new guy. He's already seeing the apparent hopelessness of our situation.

I'm not sure, but I think I learned to see a connection that's worth sharing with my peers. I tell them I don't know much about what I'm doing or where it's going. In fact, we can all stop saying that, because it's a given from herein. I am learning that the deeper I am into changing *me*, the more I see how change is going to be resisted at all angles. At first, I thought that Lora and Rick would be fully supportive of any change I implement. Now I know better. They hired coaches for us without fully understanding the consequences. They are thinking we can become agile leaders and an agile organization within the current culture and the current mindsets. That we can implement a transformational thing using the established methods and minds.

"I see your connection, Joel. It makes sense. But that is still going to be a lot of trouble for us," Meryll warns. "I don't like being the downer, here—"

"Please," Jack sighs. "You love it. You've been an alarmist from the onset of this coaching. You can't be so afraid, Meryll."

"But this is your career on the line. If Lora buries any of us, we are done. Maybe we should get some clarity from her and Rick about how our performance and coaching are tied together."

"Do you think that will make a difference?" Jack asks. "In fact, Meryll, if you had a written contract, do you think it would make a difference in the end?"

Meryll is silent and looks at the floor.

"Right." Jack affirms. "It doesn't matter. It's uncomfortable to say it, but we all work for that kind of leader. There is no trust, no accountability. As I see it, I'm at a crossroads of my career at WL. I have nothing to lose by changing my calendar, or anything else."

"So, what are you going to do about it?" Meryll is in a low place, and still she wants to take action. She comes across as negative, but her fighting spirit is really unstoppable.

"I've been thinking about that this week," Jack shrugs. "Hell, I've been thinking about it since I started here. I can't stand where things are right now, and I can't stand where *I* am right now. In fact, I'm so unhappy that I am hungry for change. But all is not lost!" He holds up an index finger. "Now that I have access to professional coaching, I'm going to use it for all I can. I'm going to get every last drop out of it, no matter the consequences at WL. I will practice everything I can. I want to be better for me far more than I want to be better for WL. In the end, if I get fired, I will have had access to some great coaching, and great practice. I want to keep an open mind about working here, while I'm still new. I plan to assess my job here every three months, and see if it still makes sense to stay. If things get really bad, I walk."

"Two feet rule," I say. "We all have two feet, so if we don't like it, we can leave."

"Yep." Jack sighs.

"It's not fair though, because *they* are the ones who stink. I mean, well, we stink too, but if we get all this coaching and become better leaders, but they stay the same, that's so unfair. They should get coaching too, and commit to change. If not, then they should get out," Meryll trails off.

Francie Van Wirkus

"Right. They stay the same," Jack says. "Maybe they will change, but we can't expect that just because they sent us to coaching. WL is not the ideal world. The fact that we are all still here shows that we all let go of the ideal a long time ago. So, now that I've put myself in this hole, I'm going to get myself out."

"It isn't fair, Meryll. And, it's feels good that you care about us. But what about working here has ever been fair? The distrust. The holding back of information, like this lean thing. Then there is shutting down Jack in meetings, and treating you so poorly that you are fearful of…most things. None of this is how leaders grow. Or, how anyone grows."

"It's so depressing," Meryll huffs. "Somehow I let all of this happen to me. Half of it, I didn't even notice until it was too late. My calendar…"

Jack nods his head. "I'm not proud or happy about where I am right now, but I'm willing to get fired if it means I can get better. That's what I've learned the last week."

Driving home that day, I couldn't help but rewind the conversation with Meryll and Jack. Especially Jack's words about his career. He inspired me to think outside my job, too. I have a lot of years at WL, but that doesn't mean I have to stay here. The thought of changing jobs isn't fun, but where I'm at right now isn't, either.

I try to picture what it would be like to leave WL for a new company. What if I pick a company that isn't as financially strong as WL? I have kids and a mortgage. On the other hand, what if I find a company that has trust and respect within its leadership ranks? I could grow exponentially. That's the kind of thinking I need to use. No assumptions about staying at WL, and no assumptions that a company can't be better than WL.

Would it be better to work in a job that stresses me out and doesn't allow for me to grow, or to be in a new job, where everything is uncertain? Up until now, I didn't think I was choosing anything. Now, slowly, my eyes are opening to my current environment, and it's clear that there is always a choice.

Reflections

Working at WL doesn't have to be forever.

I don't think I see yet all that has been holding me back.

Mostly, I have been holding myself back by being inattentive.

Francie Van Wirkus

Baby Zebra

It's a monthly director team meeting, with all of Rick's direct reports. There are about 25 of us gathered for the next two hours to get alignment on what's going on at WL. I thought it was going to be another sleeper of a meeting, where Lora and her peers strut their tail feathers for Rick. Until I begin hearing the word *resources*. *Our resources* this, and *get some resources* that. Holy crap; it's flying out of everyone's mouths except for me, Jack, and Meryll, because I shared with them my breakthrough project that morning. Jack didn't think it was a big deal, but Meryll got on board right away. Sure, she freaked out about it, but she was more curious than freaked out, and so she agreed to join in the breakthrough.

The three of us were fully engaged in the discussion; we just weren't using the "r" word. I tried not to look at either Jack or Meryll, but then I couldn't resist. That's because I could feel their eyes boring holes in me. When my eyes meet Jack's, they have an intense, knowing look. He didn't think the "r" word was a big deal, but it looks like his opinion has changed. Trying to be discrete, I make a note, and then look over at Meryll. She had been waiting to meet my eyes. What I saw in them was a real treat: for the first time, I see a sparkle of energy. She is seeing something new and getting behind it, I just know it. I relish this moment as silently as I can.

The meeting drones on. I can barely sit still because I am so uncomfortable with everyone using the 'r' word. I can't wait to tell Eve how my eyes were opened. But she already knows. Because she's probably corrected 50 people on it in her career.

However good I felt at the beginning of this meeting, I was losing it. The victory of revelation for Jack and Meryll was quickly stifled. I began to have a feeling of dread. Listen to these people. These are *my* peers. How am I going to change? It's me against my inner caveman, and everyone else's too. It's like being asked to stop swearing, when everyone else around you continues to do it. Well, there is plenty of swearing going on in the room, but with Eve's challenge, *resources* is the most offensive word of the moment. Even if Jack and Meryll are on board, this is an incredible task.

We haven't even gotten to the part of the meeting where Lora's voice gets shrill and she talks over some other director, in the name of "giving them background information."

Don't get me wrong- I am not thinking I am better than this group. I am just one of them who had my eyes opened. I'm just beginning to see the environment I've been working in for hours, weeks, months, years…this is my culture. It's starting to feel like it stinks. No wonder I stink. Did I stink when I began my leader career here? Did WL stink then too? Or was it a gradual progression, as WL grew exponentially, did we lose sight of the things that matter most, our people?

At one point in the meeting, CIO Rick asks Jack to offer his thoughts on the situation. He was the newest director in the room, and his prior experience was valuable to the discussion. None of the other directors had the specific experience that Jack did. He offered a thoughtful response, backing it up with an example from his former employer, one of our greatest competitors.

I couldn't help but look over at Lora and her peer, Gabriel. Sure enough, they are squirming and ready to pounce. They have a side conversation that lasts long enough for others to notice. Lora is almost always the one to start these, but Gabriel doesn't seem to mind. This time, Rick looks over at them, and they stop.

That's when Gabriel begins his *shake it* performance. It's what he does when he wants to speak, but knows he shouldn't be speaking. Unlike Lora, who speaks whenever she wants, no matter the consequences.

Gabriel leans back in his chair, and his knee begins bobbing up and down. Then, he leans forward on the table and both knees are rapidly bobbing. He says nothing, but then his entire body shakes in his chair. Lora is too busy worrying about what she is going to say to be bothered by him. The director on his other side notices it, but works to ignore it. What else to do when trapped at the conference table for two hours?

The group asked Jack a few more questions, and there was a healthy exchange. This is what these meetings are for, and it feels good. But it's short lived, because then it was time for the dominatrix to rear her head.

Lora literally interrupts Jack with a pointing index finger, stating she would like to offer the group context. Meryll and I lock eyes and brace for what is next. We know, because it happens in every single meeting we have with Lora. I'm sure other directors are bracing for the same thing. We can't be the only ones affected by her dominant presence. You see, Lora can't just disagree with others, she has to be *right*. She has to lead everyone around until they see it her way. She doesn't care if she has all the data or facts around the problem; she uses her world to solve everything. Being a narcissist, no one understands it all as good as she does.

In dominatrix mode, her victims are not only shut down, they are made to look small, and unaware of reality. Be assured there is zero pleasure elicited from this kind of dominatrix by anyone in the room but her. She doesn't need whips, chains, or any of that garbage to control the room. When this domination happens once, it's obnoxious and perplexing. When it happens to a victim more than once, it turns into something else. For me, it's exhausting. She's done it to me hundreds of times; I know I'm a better leader and person than she makes me feel. But every time it happens, a small part of me breaks away from her. That small piece is respect. How many pieces can break away before our relationship is permanently damaged? Never mind. It already is permanently damaged. The question now is…how many pieces can break away before *I* break away?

The other thing that really doesn't make sense is that Lora wants to be agile. How can she even understand how agile might fit at WL? She's forced us into coaching, but she's only "looking for a coach." And what happens when we get miles down the road in our agile coaching, and she's still stuck in her old world? I do: she'll smoosh agile, and us along with it. I have to remember to ask Eve about it. Well, to tell her. Eventually, my breakthrough projects are going to hit the wall of Lora.

Because this problem happens so often, and has been accepted in our culture, I don't always notice when it happens. I'm not asleep at the wheel; I'm numb to it. Often, someone else in the meeting notices it, or has been victim to it, and will come up to me later to complain about it. Or at least ask about it. All different kinds of directors. The nice ones beat themselves up and ask me if they were too this or too that in the meeting. Should they try and meet with her and get to know her better? Ah, if only it were about connection. The mean ones just call her a bitch. That's a simple problem, too. The strong ones ask me why she does it. Is she that insecure that she has to leave her scent of domination, and prove her positional power in every meeting? As if knowing the answer would somehow stop her.

In a few short sentences, Lora completely discounted Jack's experience, saying that at WL, things are different. Oops, she did it again. Jack doesn't back down immediately, and so he walks right into her trap. Well, either way, he will be in her trap. Say nothing to counter her "insight," and you instantly fade away. Push your point in an attempted sensible discussion, and you will be buried by her power in front of the group. The room begins to feel tense, but it's nothing they haven't experienced. In fact, they are all probably thinking about how this is the sacrificial offering of the New Guy.

Why would anyone try to stop it when they know the outcome? Besides, if the CIO isn't bothered by it, what could the directors do to possibly get her to change? The real irony is that she hired many of us. Yes, this is the woman who hired Jack for his "awesome outside experience." But now that he's in the door, his experience and professional mind are neutered to her (and WL's) liking.

Her voice begins low and slow, and then becomes louder as the exchange continues. Jack is the baby zebra on the African Serengeti, about to be slaughtered by the cheetah. We are all guilty for letting him be attacked, but it's safer than going in to try and help him. Jack finally catches on to what's happening to him, and shuts down. Lora's shrill voice is still echoing in the room, which is now silent. The score: baby zebra zero; Lora 1,958. Then, Rick begins with the next agenda item.

Reflections

Lora is infecting WL.

Our CIO is blind to bad behaviors.

How will agile work with bad leaders?

Mr. GQ

I'm packing up my desk, and getting ready to head over to J&L's café, when Lora is at my door.

"Joel, got a minute?" She has already stepped into my office. Apparently I do have a minute.

"Sure. I've got ten minutes before I have a hard stop to get to agile coaching."

"Great." She smiles but her face doesn't match it. Her eyes are roaming around my office instead of on me. Interesting response. The words agile coaching bothered her on some level. "What's up with your Mr. GQ wardrobe?"

"What do you mean?" I am not going to hand myself over on a platter. She's going to have to work for it. Besides, then I have more time to figure out what to say to her.

She clears her throat. "I've noticed lately that you're going pretty…casual."

"Oh. Is there a concern about it?"

"I'm just curious why the sudden change?" Her arms are folded in her crisp, Escada suit. "I noticed Jack wasn't wearing a suit, either."

I'm tempted to tell her I ran out of dry cleaning budget. "It's an agile coaching assignment. I want to be more accessible to my…teams." Damn, I almost said resources. *Take that, inner caveman!*

"Huh." Lora is completely thrown by this answer. "I thought you were working on your calendar? And why is Jack involved?"

"I am working on my calendar. More of that to come," I assure her. "As far as Jack, maybe you should ask him."

Lora's eyes show her mind going to a thousand places at once. "So, no more suits?" Her hand is under her chin, but her index finger points and sweeps up and down at me. *She's winding up for the pitch…*

"I will wear them when it's the best choice. I'll also wear these fine clothes when it's the best choice." I smooth over my Express cashmere sweater. It's the closest thing to comfort I've worn to work in my entire career.

"Can I offer you some insight?" *And the pitch. A line drive…*God, for once in my life do I stop her? But if I do stop her, then…ahk, it's too late. I have to respond.

"Sure, if you can do it in less than seven minutes. Otherwise, we can talk later."

"I know you're trying to listen to your agile coach, and I think that's great. I really believe in the process, or I wouldn't have sponsored it for you." *More like shoved me into it.*

"But Joel, just remember that they have no idea what it's like to work here. They may not understand the matrixed organization you lead, or the culture. You're getting advice that might not work at WL. You know, these coaches have a lot of big ideas to boil the ocean and change the world. Sustainable change doesn't happen like that." Lora picks a piece of lint or some microscopic organism off her lapel. "I hate to see you get all jazzed about something you learned in coaching and not be able to use it here. You'll have to balance the advice and coaching you get with the reality at WL. It's not going to be easy, but I know you're up to the challenge."

This is rich on so many levels. With just two minutes left, I can't go anywhere with this conversation.

"Thanks Lora."

"Just because Rick didn't notice what you were wearing doesn't mean it's okay."

"It's not okay to wear this?" I'm standing now, getting my coat on.

Lora shrugs. "I didn't say it wasn't *okay*, I just wonder if it's the best change for our culture."

I have to leave so I'm not late for Eve. Add poetry to my leader skills. Mr. GQ-The-Poet. "Lora, thanks for your good thoughts. I've got to run."

Lora, all-knowing leader of the universe, nods, "It's about *balance*, Joel."

Reflections

Lora wants to change agile for it to fit into WL.

Like Cele said, I am cuter in business casual menswear.

Now What?

"Nice sweater, Joel." Eve grins as she opens her mini laptop. She always looks good, but today she is wearing a green scarf that sets her eyes on fire.

"Thank you, Eve," I demur. "It's nice of you to notice. In fact, you're not the only one who noticed." I tell her about Lora's impromptu visit and (now infamous) *offer of insight*.

"You're scaring her already, Joel."

"I thought maybe *you* were the scary one because you are the coach."

"To clarify, you are beginning to represent change, and change scares her."

I sit back with my arms folded. "I told you so."

"Right, and we are not going to spend our entire time together talking about Lora. We could talk about her until the end of time, but this is Joel Time." She gives me a fist bump. "Let's talk about your last breakthrough project, the one where you completely stop calling people *resources*, and you get Jack and Meryll on board for it too."

"All I have to say is…wow. I had no idea how many times I say that damn word, and I sure didn't realize how prolific it was in our company." I tell her about the director meeting with our CIO, and how it stunned me, and how Jack and Meryll were freaking out in there, too. She laughed.

"Nice work bringing Jack and Meryll along with you. Are you cured of it?"

"I'm really trying not to say it. I'm probably 90% not using it. Jack and Meryll are definitely going to help me. We will catch each other at it, even if just for sport." I sip my house blend. "Sometimes I feel really good about what we are doing here. I can see the connections. But sometimes I feel like I don't have enough direction on where we are going."

Eve uses her best German accent, "You are hungry for more! You want to learn agile!"

I roll my eyes. "You're not going to teach me agile today. But I am hungry for knowing where this is all going."

"We are building you into a good leader, who over time can become a great leader. While you're working on being a great leader, we'll teach you to be an agile leader."

"I keep waiting for it."

"Maybe next time we meet I'll give you a tool box with a hammer and a mess of nails in it." Eve looks away.

"What does that mean, that I'm a tool head? I'm not, really."

"You are, Joel. You keep asking about agile like it's one of those boxes of organic tea behind the counter over there."

She should see the people I work with. I am a rebel compared to them. "Can you at least tell me when we get to something that is close to agile?"

Eve chuckles. "Someday you will see it, Joel. Until then, most of where this is going is up to you. You could take Lora's approach, which means you don't believe you or WL can fully change. Ever. Or you could take an open minded approach. Trust me and then experiment with some of it."

"Experiment." I know it's lame, but I picture myself in a hazardous materials suit.

"Yes. Plan it, do it, check it, adjust it. We have started a few experiments already, Joel. Can you tell me what they are?"

I'm pretty sure I get the concept. "My calendar changes?"

Eve nods yes.

"My wardrobe change, even though Karen helped reveal that one to me, not you."

"Yes. What about the permanent change to stop using the word resources for people?"

"Uh, no, because it's permanent. Not an experiment."

"Right. We could really get into the topic of experiments, but let's not dive too far into that today." Eve assures me we will get to that topic eventually.

She offers that I can research it on my own if I like, but it's not an assignment. She made some comment about it keeping me from getting bored. I assured her that the assignments she has given me so far in combination with working for Lora will keep me from getting bored. I'm not sure what the big deal is. Trying something and then deciding if it worked? Sounds like fifth grade science class. If Eve's going to teach it to me, there is no way it's going to be easy.

We talk about *go & see* again. Eve tells me it's time to add another building block to it. Now that I've started to visit my teams, removed the word *resources* from my vocabulary, and made myself a little more approachable with my clothing choices, I can do more. I get what Eve is doing now. Her approach is saving my ass from failure and basic embarrassment. I tell her this with gratitude, and she laughs at me.

"You are beginning to catch on."

"I still stink, don't I?"

Eve nods. "Pretty much. But don't feel bad. We are going to rock this."

"Right." I roll my eyes. "First you mock me for stinking it up, then you tell me it's not that bad."

"You are making great progress, so let's keeping building on it. Can you find the gemba questions you wrote in your notebook?"

I open to the page:

What are you trying to do?

Can you show me how you currently do this?

Can you show me what's frustrating about your current process?

"Your breakthrough project is to actually start practicing *go & see* with these questions." Eve taps her hand on my notebook. "You're ready. Just relax."

Francie Van Wirkus

"Right. Relax." Change how I think and how I lead, but relax.

Reflections

I need to know more about experiments.

When I change, I can scare others just by what I represent.

Go & see is complicated!

I love getting home by 5:30 p.m.

Just Putting up with it

Eve and I have a special session this week, just to debrief the director team meeting I wrote about earlier. You know, the one where Lora was the dominatrix-cheetah, and Jack the baby zebra on the African Serengeti? That one.

Eve thought it would be a good idea to debrief it for a few reasons. She wanted a better view into the kind of people I work with, to see my common work situations, so she can coach me from their mistakes. I guess. Why make up a coaching situation when you can pick apart one that really happened?

I'm sure Eve has a pretty good idea what most corporate environments are like, but I liked that she wanted to learn more about mine. I'm new to agile coaching, but I believe a good coach wants to know the details, and doesn't assume a lot. I liked how she cared enough to give this meeting an entire session. How sad though, that we have to take our time to debrief all the bad things that happened in just one meeting.

Instead of going through the play-by-play of Lora's bad behavior, we use my reflection notes as starting place.

Eve said we weren't reviewing it to figure out how to fix all of the problems, but to look for connections and opportunities. Here are my notes:

Reflections

Lora is infecting WL.

Our CIO is blind to bad behaviors.

How will agile work with bad leaders?

"Joel, what do you think are the core issues with your first note, that Lora's bad leadership is infecting WL?" Eve asks.

"Wouldn't it be *Lora* who is the core issue of Lora?"

"Yes." Eve agrees with the obvious. "And, if you could have seen what she was thinking in that meeting, what do you think you'd see?"

"I hate to guess."

"You've worked with her long enough; you're not guessing." Eve's persistent, green eyes dig into mine. "You know who she is. Is it hard to admit you work for someone like this?"

I'm uncomfortable. I didn't want to go to that place, but here we are. "You hit a nerve, Eve. I can't believe I've been working for her for so long, just putting up with it." I tell Eve that the first year I worked for Lora, I thought it was me. I didn't know Lora was a narcissist then, so I honestly thought most problems were my fault. *If only I had done this, if only that...*

The next few years, I figured out that I wasn't to blame for everything, but that still left the problem of Lora. I got advice now and then from a friend and read many leadership books along the way, but nothing changed. Meaning, I didn't change my situation. I didn't confront Lora (who would?!). I didn't look for a new job. Sometimes I just rolled over and let her do whatever she wanted. I did develop some great coping skills. If I were to train someone else on how to do my job, it would mostly be coping activities to work with Lora.

"Let's look at a higher level than Lora's mind. What might be some other reasons she is infecting the organization?"

I read my notes again, as if that helps. I answer Eve that it's mostly Rick. It's hard to say if he is aware of how Lora infects her teams or not. A reasonable person would assume he is aware of it. She reports to him. He works with her often, in all sorts of settings. Still, wouldn't you think that a well-intentioned guy like him would put a stop to it, if he was aware of it? Maybe he's ignoring her. Does he hold onto her because she is intelligent (she is)? Is there some other value he believes she offers?

"Which brings us right to your second point, there."

"Yes. I guess I assumed that he doesn't see the damage she is causing."

"Is it only her?"

"No. Her bad behavior is the most obvious, but there are plenty of other things happening around us. Hoarding re—uh, *people* for pet projects," I pause to make sure she hears me use the right word. Her face lights up. Victory, albeit very small.

"Also, directors are good at holding things back when they don't get what they want, not helping New Guy Jack get on board, and putting up with Lora."

Eve asks me what I think about Rick's leadership. I think she already knows the answer, but she is forcing me to look at the way we work.

"Look, I could speculate all day about what Rick's issues are, but where does that get us, Eve? I wrote these reflections down, but I don't expect a clear answer for how to fix all of them."

Eve sighs. "So, it's hopeless."

"Well who are you coaching, me or Rick or Lora?"

"I love that you are asking me, although in a very roundabout way, *what problem are we trying to solve?*"

"That's it. What are we doing here today? It's a huge, complicated mess. What is the part I can impact?"

"Right. A great question in any situation. In fact, agile leaders are always asking themselves, *what question should I be asking right now*? For you, in this big mess, you can't go wrong with asking *what problem am I trying to solve?*"

She's making me crazy again. "Eve, I get what you're saying, but you're not answering my question."

Eve shrugs. She is far less exhausted from today's journey than I am. "It was a great coaching opportunity. I couldn't resist."

"We reward heroics. You know, drive for results, press on, and lead the teams down the field. Our performance management system is set up to support all of this behavior. So as much as Rick is part of the problem, it's a deep, matrixed situation."

Eve agrees with me, but says nothing more. I think it's because she has led us to a place and I'm supposed to know where we are.

"This is the part where I ask about how these inherited bad behaviors work with agile, right?"

Eve's smile says it all. Once in a while, when Eve is not annoying me, I have these moments of guilt that I'm spending time in a café with another beautiful woman. Now is one of those moments. It's fleeting, gone before I really notice it. That's because the giant, dysfunctional things we are talking about are so overwhelming.

"So you are the agile expert, not me."

"It's your reflection, not mine."

"Touché."

Eve laughs. "Let's look at it this way, Joel. We've worked on just a few things so far, real tip-of-the-iceberg sort of stuff. You're cleaning up your calendar, looking for where you add value, beginning to spend time with your teams, and beginning to increase your respect for them. Do you think that if there were no impending agile transformation out there, these changes would still make you and WL better right now?"

"Of course."

There is silence. That's because once again, I have my answer. She's walked me right to it again, like a professional. At least Lora and Rick hired a good coach for me. I can't believe I'm saying it, but my time with Eve has been incredibly difficult and great, all at once. I've gone from being angry about having to come to these sessions, to looking forward to them. Eve is absolutely in my head for me to be my best.

Back to the topic at hand; I really am a crappy leader. I'm one of many. It's so depressing. Yes, I'm doing something about it by meeting with Eve, but I have my doubts how it's all going to work out. WL is so complicated, so intertwined, how could we ever get everyone to change?

"Exactly." Eve catches the doubt on my face. "But you have doubts."

"Yes. Don't you?"

"Yes." Eve finishes her matcha. "Let's bring this session home, Joel. Tell me about the last time a big change was introduced in your area. There was bad leadership back then. What happened after the change?"

I share with her the last time we were reorganized about three years ago. There was all sorts of dysfunction happening at my level and at the manager level. Isn't that just part of what happens when you tear up a division and rebuild it? Eve said no, it could be done in a way that is chaotic, but feels positive.

Anyway, Rick was the new CIO. Part of the reorganization required shoring up a bunch of people for the work. And there was a process that was used. You know, search for the available, qualified person, send the list to the managers who need people, then the manager selects a person, then the person confirms his or her acceptance, and then the assignment is recorded.

There were quite a few problems with the process. Rick heard about it and got involved. Maybe because he was new, I don't know. He got in the weeds on the process and saw "a gap." So he removed the step in the process that the people accept the assignment. He said people cannot refuse an assignment. I think many managers breathed a sigh of relief that they could just rack and stack their *resources*. But it felt weird to many of us.

The very same day, I worked with Rick on a communication about the reorg. It was so ironic; Rick wanted to "make sure we had a good communication plan, so our teams feel they are in charge of their own destinies."

"Well." Eve sits back with her arms folded. "That's rich. We will use this story again in the future to talk about trust. For now, let's apply it to what we were talking about. Wow, it's hard to keep this straight!"

"My turn to laugh. It's twistedly comforting to know that you are bothered by the amount of stuff we have to talk about."

"It happens." Eve throws up her hands.

"So, bad leadership happened. Did it matter that it was a reorganization or that Rick was new?"

"No."

"Right. It didn't matter then, and it doesn't matter now. It can be the introduction of agile, a reorganization, a downsize event, whatever. It's the culture at WL. It will transcend all of those events."

I put my head in my hands. Culture. Of course.

"We will not touch culture today, so you can relax. It's a huge topic with agile, and we will do it justice. But not today."

"Thank you."

"No breakthrough project today, because you already have one." Eve smiles as if she's giving me a huge gift.

I guess this is sort of a nice gift. I'm still trying to get my head around our last meeting and the ask-three-questions-breakthrough project. What really bothers me is the fact that I need someone to feed me questions to better connect with my team. It's embarrassing and humbling to have this assignment, even when Eve doesn't make me feel this way. Shouldn't I have been asking these questions of my teams and managers all along? And, asking them in person? Why haven't I been doing this with them? Because it hasn't been expected of me.

I'm fully confident that I'm going to screw it up, but I'm going to try it anyway. I can't expect to push past all of this by just talking about it. The feeling is remarkably similar to having a new job. How about that.

Reflections

Culture change sounds huge.

I don't know much about what I'm supposed to be doing.

I am ready to change.

Capacity

Meryll was right. Lora didn't have a clue about how dramatic of a change we made to our schedules. To complicate matters, she couldn't find me to confront me about it. I was busy spending time with my teams, executing my breakthrough project. More on that later. Although I have to say, it has been a really good experience.

I get an instant message from Lora wondering where I am. She wrote that she had been looking for me most of the morning, and that I was "really hard to find." It reminds me of when I was young, when my brother and I were out and about in the neighborhood and our mother was trying to find us. *"Where have you boys been? Don't you know I've been looking all over for you?"*

I want to text something snarky back to her like, it's not her turn to watch me, but I skip past it. This new way I'm working is going to be so difficult for her. I'm not muddying the waters with sarcasm or crap responses. I need simply tell her the truth.

She insists that we need to talk today, so I offer her a 30 minute time slot this afternoon. Of course we were going to talk today. What did she think I was going to do, run away from her? Oh, right, she already thinks I'm avoiding her, so yeah, she believes I will do more of the same. Anyway, 30 minutes is enough; we do not need an hour for me to get slammed by her for whatever is the current problem.

As the day goes on, the usual feeling of dread I have for these sorts of interaction is there, but today there is more. It's a deep feeling of...bad. I'm not sure what it's all about. Thoughts of Eve, Rick and Lora, and things Meryll has said are all swirling around in my head. It's a mess of things. A nice run outside would help clear things, but I can't break away today. I leave the feeling alone, and focus on what's in front of me.

As I walk to our meeting spot, I imagine that Eve is walking with me. She'd offer me encouragement, and then she'd have a profound question like, why are you meeting with her? Of course I wouldn't know the reason other than that's the way we've always done it. Then we'll go into some discussion that ends up with me doing something completely the opposite of how I currently lead. But she's not here, so I'm going to have to try to relax and do my best to handle whatever Lora is so concerned about.

Lora arrives seven minutes late, which is rather early for her. How did I wait for her before we had smart phones and tablets?

"Joel, I wanted to talk with you about your capacity."

"What's up?" I try to be light. It's going to be about my calendar. *Here's the windup...*

"I was on the weekly conference call with the user experience team but you weren't on." *And the pitch...*

"I'm not needed on that call, Lora. I've repurposed the time to lead my teams." I'm speaking just a little too fast. Slow it down. "It's part of my assignment from agile coaching."

"What do you mean *you're not needed on the call*? Did they tell you that?" *A solid hit to center field!* Lora's voice is already getting tight. This is really bothering her.

"I told them. We had a good discussion about it. They know I am here for them if they need me," I said. Then I reminded Lora of the calendar discussion Jack, Meryll and I had with her and Rick. Once again, I explained to her the activity of looking at what meetings and interactions I add value to and which ones I don't. The user experience team meeting is too in the weeds for me to be attending each week.

"That's ridiculous." Lora is hearing it all for the first time. Somewhere at WL, Meryll is nodding her head saying *I told you she wasn't listening.* "You can't just...stop attending that call, Joel. I'm still on it."

"Maybe you can't Lora, but I did an intentional exercise that helped me see where I add value. It was interesting that the user experience project manager agreed that I didn't need to attend the meeting every week. He knows that I'm happy to attend in the future when there is a special circumstance."

"That PM isn't very strong. He's happy you're no longer holding him accountable," Lora huffs.

"I wasn't holding him accountable. I was supposed to be looking for cross functional alignment opportunities. At least, that's what your vision was for my involvement with this conference call, and the five others you assigned me to." So much for my work in building trust with Lora.

Lora pauses for a moment. "Let's say I'm not on the call, and you're not on the call. What happens when that team needs our perspective? What happens when they need our perspective and they *don't know* they need it?" Lora isn't really asking me. "It will be a lost opportunity."

"That's what I thought, Lora. Then I took time to do some honest reflection on the value I add in that meeting. The reality is, they don't need me there."

It's clear Lora's had enough, and we're only 15 minutes into our meeting, including the seven minutes she was late. "I have to run. Can you please send me a report of all the meetings you are skipping, and why? I might need to see how we can cover this while you're in coaching."

"Lora, this isn't a temporary thing. I don't intend to rejoin that meeting."

Her nose twitches. This means she is really mad. I've seen it many times before. "Well, send me the report anyway. I need to get a handle on what is going on."

"I would like it better if we talked about it. I had a really great discussion with my coach that I'd like to share with you. That might be more valuable for both of us than a report."

"Let's do both," she commands. "What's with you using the word "value" all of the time?"

I know her so well. She really doesn't want an answer to this question. But I also know that I can't avoid the question. I have to walk into it and pretend she cares about what I'm going to say. If Eve and I keep working together, there are probably going to be a lot of conversations like this one in the future. I might as well begin practicing them now.

"I'm glad you asked, Lora." That sounded lame. I can do better. I must do better. "Value is a big part of the discussion I had with my coach. In fact, she's earned my respect since we started talking about value. She really opened my eyes to getting a better look at what's going on around me. Progress and impediments—"

"We'll talk about it sometime." This is too much for her. She checks her phone and gets up to leave. "Send me that report," she calls over her shoulder.

Driving home that night, that bad feeling came back even stronger. I fantasize about what it might be like to be retired. I think of hiking trails in the mountains, swimming pools, and beaches, like Cele's parents' place out in Oregon. Lots of sunsets, oceans, walks, and peace. Cele and I will have our differences, but the stress of any of our disagreements is nothing compared to the stress of a disagreement with Lora.

I laugh at myself. Here I am, trying to forget the dysfunction of being a leader by fantasizing about being retired. I probably have 20 years before I can do that. If things don't change, I might die trying. That's not in the plans. What happened to the days when I was energized by work? In fact, when *was* the last time I was energized by what I do? What a depressing state I'm in. Don't feel sorry for me, as I've had free will and choices all along. I wasn't looking at the right things, and I have a flawed vision of what it means to be a leader.

With a few miles to wrestle with the noise in my head, it's now clear what this bad feeling is: Lora has no idea why she hired a coach for us. For whatever reason she shoved us into it, it's not because she understands agile. Even more depressing, she doesn't believe she has to change. Only other people around her. I'll never know how she was influenced or inspired to get agile coaching for us. She probably stole a list from some agile blog, took the things that sounded good, and then made a list for herself. Put Meryll, Joe and Jack in coaching. *Check!*

If she doesn't know why we are being coached, and doesn't think she needs coaching, I am screwed. And, I am guessing, so is the pending agile transformation at WL. This is what Meryll saw ahead of me and Jack. Meryll tends to be dramatic, but with this revelation, I completely understand why she's so wound up.

And I'm supposed to be working on building trust with Lora. Maybe that's not what I need at all. In the perfect world, trust would be something to work for and nurture over time. To get by in a world with Lora as my director, maybe I need to go a different route. It's a big discovery, and it's a real bummer. This broken relationship is so dysfunctional that I feel like it's all on me. I could work on building trust with her for the rest of my career and never get it.

What's the point of any of it? Why try to push through barriers that will never be broken? I remember a conversation Eve and I had. She challenged me: don't I want to be a better leader, regardless of what's going on around me? Yes, I do. That sounded inspiring at the time, and got me excited to change. But what if the environment around me no longer understands me and my agile ways (if we ever get to agile)?

Jack seemed confident that there are other companies out there who would value agile leadership. He hasn't been here forever like me, so his mind is still open to other possibilities. Well, that's the story I tell myself about why Jack can still see beyond the fence lines. I like his fresh view of things, and need to spend more time talking about the view with him. Jack, without even trying, showed me that my current view is stagnant. What a disturbing revelation, when you see that you've been asleep at the wheel of your own career. What happened? What the hell am I doing?

Over time, I have lost my ability to see myself being successful outside this company. Long ago my father had advised me: *"Work at least one level above where you are. If the people around you don't notice, don't fight it too much. Keep doing what you do, and someone else will see your value."* There is that word *value* again. So I lost sight of Dad's advice, somewhere around the time I started working for Lora. Back then, I was so eager to please her, that I contorted myself in many different directions. All the while, Lora and Rick have made me feel like I was the one who needed to better understand WL's culture and vision. I didn't have the right insight, the right perspective, or the right world view. I would be better if only I could have the same viewpoint as Lora or Rick.

I'm pulling into my driveway just as I arrive at the question, *so now what?* Can't answer that now that I'm home. Huh. Stone cold sober, I have no recollection of how I drove my car for 30 minutes to this point. Eve will have to hear about this. Listen to me, anticipating the next time I get to talk with her. I've gone from resenting my coaching assignment to wanting more help from her each day.

Reflections

My leadership team doesn't understand why the three of us are getting agile coaching.

My leadership team doesn't believe that they need to change.

I have been asleep at the wheel of my career for a very long time. It feels terrible.

Jack's fresh eyes are helpful to me. I need to spend more time with him.

I think I can change my view.

Francie Van Wirkus

To Report…or not to Report

Early the next morning, I'm swimming with the masters' swim group at my local pool. Masters swimming is a kind word for old people swimming. If you are a competitive swimmer, you are old when you turn 24. So I'm a fully qualified masters swimmer. And no, I don't wear a banana hammock. I am civilized and wear jammers. Coming here two or three times a week is the one piece of Ironman triathlon training I've been doing for a long time. Swimming might seem mind numbing, going back and forth over and over, but I get really good mental clarity during my workouts. I always feel better when I am finished. Not just because the suffering stopped, but because there is a refreshing feeling that is unique to being in the water.

During the warm up, there is a lot of noise in my head leftover from yesterday's exchange with Lora. She actually wants a stupid report about what meetings I'm "skipping" and why. By the time the warm up is over, I'm pissed and wound up. Bring on the main set.

We're swimming intervals, 14 X 200 yards, descending. This means the last ones are faster than the first ones. There are more geeky details to the set, but you get the idea: it means pain. During the first few intervals, I think about putting off the report Lora wants, just because. I know this report is wrong and wasteful, but I'm not sure on the technical reasons why. Eve would know. I could call her today and ask her. Then again, I don't want to call her for every little thing. I don't want to get too dependent on her for little things…

In the middle of the set, I get snarky and imagine a report that lists all of the meetings by name as she requested and then by the reason why I'm "skipping" them, the word WASTE. In all caps, just like that, over and over for each report listed. Ah, how that would stir conversation.

Actually, that idea sparked another that I'm going to use for this assignment. By the 14th 200, I had a plan. I'll give her the damn report today. It will take me maybe ten minutes to create it. I'll list every meeting I'm not attending on a regular basis, and then I'll list the same reason that I no longer attend them on a regular basis for all of them: *I am not adding value to this meeting.*

During our cool-down, I run through what will happen next. I expect Lora to twist my reason into a performance problem. Such as, I don't know what my role is on those calls, and I didn't ask for help to better understand them. Maybe I'm unclear about what connections and alignment opportunities are out there. More of the same narrative: *I am the problem, not the process.* I will ask Eve to help me with this part. It's a rich topic, as she would say, but there has to be one small chunk that I can try to do differently. She can find hope in what I see as hopeless.

While driving to work, I'm still thinking about the hopeless reactions to my report. Enough already. The sooner I write the damn thing and send it to her, the sooner I can clear it out of my head.

When I arrive at work, I dive right into the report and finish it in ten minutes. I hit the send button to email it to her and sigh. The day can only go up from here, right?

Reflections

The change in my calendar is a problem for my leaders.

Value sounds huge.

Culture

I'm sitting in another department's monthly director team meeting to offer alignment and perspective. I do add some value on occasion, so I kept this one on my calendar. For now. It's not the worst meeting of the month, but it's tedious. The meeting is for a group that is part of our division, but Lora's not in this meeting. Her peer, Vladimir, is. He has an even larger group of directors who report to him, maybe 10 of them, and most of them are in attendance. Anika is one of them; she is in charge of this month's meeting. She's a lovely Dutch woman who has a niche expertise. It is not, however, holding concise meetings. She beats a dead horse with the best of them, and lets others do the same. She knows how to play the WL culture game well. Her pointy, tortoise shell glasses are her best prop to pull it off.

Holding her glasses in one hand, Anika makes a few announcements about what's happening that month, and then pulls up the communication calendar on the big screen for Vlad's director team. It's available to everyone on a collaborative page, so people can read it and add to it at any time. Each event has a date, a description, location, and an owner. No matter. This meeting is two hours long, and often the first hour is gobbled up by this activity.

Anika combs through everything on the calendar for the next two months. If the owner of the meeting is in the room, he or she offers context about the event, even if it was done at the last meeting. Usually, this is the case.

What it ends up being is an opportunity for the event owner to talk in great detail about how fantastic it is that they are (insert cool tech verb here, like *leveraging*) this event for their cause. The director is usually looking at Vladimir when speaking. Often times Vlad nods his head and smiles, and then goes back to writing notes.

This week is no different. We are in Leader Validation Central. There is showboating, bragging, and jockeying for position by most of the directors. These people really, really want Vlad to know that they are working hard and solving all kinds of complicated problems. On and on it goes until we are at the end of the calendar list.

"We have a director team summit in two months, and I need some help planning it. Anyone interested?"

Crickets.

"What is the goal of it?" I ask. "Maybe that will help us."

Crickets. And questioning stares.

"What do you mean, the goal?" Anika casually asks. "It's a director summit."

Crap. That was New Joel talking. The one being coached to look for where I can add value. This room doesn't know New Joel yet. If I'm not careful, I will sound like a quality jerk.

"Yes, an all-day summit—"

"Two days." Anika interrupts. "Well, a day and a half, and then we can go to the bar." She is looking over her glasses at me with full superiority.

"Okay, two days. But why are we getting together?" *Man, hold it together. Don't say the word value…* "What are the expected…outcomes?"

"Alignment, of course." Anika smiles nervously and looks at Vladimir, who has stopped writing. She has an answer for everything, because she is the all-knowing defender, and I am the challenger. She has no idea why we are having a director summit, but since we've always done a summit in the spring, we should do a summit.

"Can anyone think of another reason we are having a summit?" Anika asks like a third grade teacher.

The room tenses; everyone else smells trouble, and so they remain neutral. Neutral crickets. Agree with Anika, and get assigned some big planning task that no one has time for. Agree with me, and it's a roll of the dice where that goes. Why pick sides if you don't have to?

"We have some vision work to do on agile," Vladimir says without looking up. "Everyone is very busy." He finally makes eye contact with us. "Anika, can you please find some resources to help us plan it? We need to keep our eyes on the ball right now."

Anika adjusts her glasses. "Yes, of course. I will tap the resources we used last year and see if they're interested." She smiles and then looks over at me. "I'm sure they would love the opportunity."

"So, we're going agile?" Chase, a veteran director, asks. I know he knew this because he attended a different meeting with me when it was a topic.

Before Vladimir can answer, Anika butts in. "Are we going to get training for that?"

"Where did you hear we are getting training?" Chase asks.

"Well, I haven't," Anika shrugs. "If we are directors of teams going agile, don't we have to get them training?"

Chase sighs. "Oh. I thought you meant that we needed training."

"I don't think so…" Anika looks at Vladimir.

"We should all go to training," Dipti adds.

And coaching! I can't believe all of this happened from one question about value. It's created discussion and discomfort, all at once. Eve is going to die when she hears this one.

Anika takes her glasses off. "I hear the training is five full days. And very expensive."

"So who's budget would that come out of? It sounds like a nightmare." Chase holds his head in his hands.

Vladimir interrupts the nervous chatter. "We are going to use agile at WL." More sighs and whispers. "Everyone calm down. This is a good thing. If you are really interested in agile, why not sign up to help plan the summit?"

Silence. Except for Anika's fingernails clacking on her laptop. She's scheduling a planning meeting for next week and inviting several staff to it.

"We will revisit agile when we have the right group in the room. In the meantime, do not send anyone to training. Do not go out ahead of what the vision is."

"What is the vision?" Chase asks.

Vladimir smiles. "I guess we have an answer to what we'll be doing at the director team summit."

Now that the calendar has been thrashed to death, we get into the lightening round. It's supposed to be a quick hit way for everyone to talk about what's going on, and it usually fuels discussion for later in the meeting. Each person talks for up to two minutes. You can research on the Internet how a real lightening round works. How it works with Vlad's team is different. For starters, it takes way longer than it should.

We're already beaten down from the calendar exercise, and with no break, a deflated room of leaders presses on to the next thing. Drive for results. Solve problems. Repeat. This is how we get aligned.

The first director to go is Dipti. She understands the lightening round, and knows how to be precise. She's finished in less than two minutes. The next director begins to speak, until Anika interrupts. She wants Dipti to give more information on what's happening. Dipti answers her first question without a lot of detail, and offers to expand on it later. Anika seems awkwardly satisfied but doesn't ask any more questions. Anika has no intentions of circling back. She only wants to look engaged and smart in front of Vlad. Dipti knows this, so instead of looking annoyed, she smiles as if she is having the time of her life. Vlad is taking notes again. Maybe writing a grocery list, it's hard to tell if he's listening or not.

It's Chase's turn. He talks about his team's accomplishments from last month and last week. It's a long list. Most don't notice that he never gets to what he's doing right now, which is, of course, the point of the lightening round. Probably because he's not really doing anything right now. He is one of the masters at talking about what needs to be done, but not actually doing anything. I forget about his mode of operation until I'm back in this meeting.

Francie Van Wirkus

After the long list of what happened in the past, Chase talks about what's going to happen next. Big things, big plans. Lots of action, action, action! Finally, he always has a story about how awesome he is. This time, one of his teams was struggling with a problem…that is, until he solved it for them. As if this is a skill that he alone possesses. If only we would listen to how he does it, we, too, could begin our journey to be as good as him.

"They're such a good group," he feigns connection, "so I always want to do the right thing for them."

Chase probably recorded his speech so he can type it and put it in his performance evaluation.

The next few directors take their turn, each talking longer than the last. Add to that Anika's questions, and it's going to be another 30 minutes before the lightening round makes its way to me. I am going to be the last person to go, unless there is a late arrival. Fine by me. While I'm waiting, I think about what are my top three things I am working on this week? Getting shredded by Lora? Writing a dumb meetings report for Lora?

I check my watch. The hopeful part of me wants to share New Joel with the team, you know, what I'm doing to change the way I lead. I don't know what I'm doing at all, but that is part of the story. I'm in a fog, but making my way one step at a time. I'm really excited about making a change and think most directors there would be interested in learning more. *I'm looking to add value.* They would be uncomfortable and Anika would ask about 3,000 questions, but I could see it being a positive thing. There is so much to share, but this is not the time. It would freak everyone out. The real problem, however, is where things are at with Lora. She is making me I feel like I'm a rebel faction within the company. If I start talking about it to others, I'll be nailed for stirring up the troops. So I'll stick to talking about some vendor agreements I'm working on, and call it a day.

Just before it's my turn, Anika interrupts. "Oops, we went over a bit."

Everyone looks at their watches.

"I think Joel still has a turn," she smiles at me. I smile back. I'm having the time of my life.

"Since we're just about out of time," she looks at me over her fancy glasses, "can you please make sure you keep your status *under two minutes*?" Anika speaks to me as if she's identified the problem with going over, and I am the problem.

"Sure." I keep smiling. "The three things I want to accomplish this week are…"

Thankfully, no one asked me any questions. That's because they were all in a meeting coma. The tail end of the meeting has deflated because the room is exhausted. Yes, the lightening round was more like a land tortoise round.

This derailment happens in many meetings like this one. The first part of "let's go around the room" over-reaches what it's supposed to accomplish. Deep dives in minutia, extra conversations, rabbit holes, sidebar conversations, whatever you want to call them.

These derailments happen for all different reasons, but mostly because the directors are showing off their tail feathers. Who is the smartest one? Who has the coolest project? Who has the most "resources" reporting to them? And, because there was no real focus for our gathering. I'm just guessing that long ago, alignment was probably a burning platform for our teams. Some terrible communication misstep probably happened, and the VPs were up in arms about it. That's usually how it works at WL.

When the memory of the problem blows over, the meeting remains, and it is just another required appearance. Someone is in charge of the agenda, and it's their job to fill it for every meeting. If it's been a two hour meeting in the past, it will remain a two hour meeting indefinitely. Headcount in the meeting doesn't vary too much either. The new director simply inherits all of the meetings of the former director, without any questions asked. Don't forget! The need to fit in and start adding value is strong, so the sooner the new leader speaks up in these meetings, the better. Vocal means engaged, even if the leader is simply parroting back something someone else said.

No one challenges any part of this approach. I don't know other leaders' reasons for not suggesting change, but mine is that I don't want to look like I don't care. I want to look like I am an engaged leader who just loves to make connections across the organization. Then there is the fact that I'm moving so fast, I forget about the dysfunction in this meeting until I'm in it again. *Oh, that's right. This meeting stinks because we waste time.*

In the end, the topics that were missed, like my status, are usually swept under the rug, or postponed for "next time." Instead of fixing the flaws of the meeting, people cope with them. There is jockeying to go first in meetings, so your burning issue is sure to get its time with the teams. Then there are the leaders who only show up when they have something "really important" to share with the group. And there is the meeting after the meeting. All those hours wasted in this meeting, and others like it, and yet we don't have enough time to fix them. Or rather, don't take the time to fix them.

I'll have to be sure and thank Eve for introducing me to the concept of value. Now I'm conflicted by the hour with the waste I see around me. It's as if here at WL, we don't expect value.

Reflections

Leaders are worried.

I see things I have not seen before.

Value is not an expectation at WL.

My Worst One

Eve told me I was ready to *go & see* and ask questions, but I don't think I am ready. I've changed how I dress, stopped saying the word *resources* when I mean people, and memorized the three questions. I'm coached just enough to be dangerous.

Once again, I choose to begin in Vijay and Karen's area. I've checked their calendars to look for the best day and time to visit the team. I pick Thursday morning and I'm nervous as hell. What if all the cell phones start vibrating again? What if they don't answer the questions? Worse yet, what if I don't ask the questions properly? What if they ask me something and I don't know the answer?

Enough hesitation. I want to be a better leader, and an agile leader. I'm trusting Eve when she tells me that practicing this will help me be both. I am going to go through with it, even if it's my worst ever attempt at leading. Just dive in.

"So, how's it going?" I'm at Karen's cube.

"Good." Karen greets me as she stands up. "What's up?"

"Just visiting. Not checking up on you, just seeing if there is anything you need my help with."

Karen smiles. "Ah, that's right. You are doing *go & see*. Well, in that case, I want to show you something."

That was easy.

We don't stay at her desk long enough to hear if her phone is getting texts from the team. I'm glad, because I can't worry about that right now. I have to focus on *go & see!* Karen leads me to the desk of a re—team member I haven't met before, Chris. Karen introduces us, and then she asks him to show me the research summary he made on corporate collaboration sites. That's right, we were going to get one of those, but then it fell out of priority when WL was focused on buying another company. I try to remember who had accountability for this, but I can't remember. Besides, I need to focus on what Chris is showing me.

Chris was on his *go & see* game. He doesn't drone on and on with what he did; he shows me that he did the research, and then asks me, "Who can we share this research with in a way that will get some traction?"

"So, what are you trying to do?" I ask. I'm sweating but more importantly, I'm interested in what Chris is asking me.

"Like, the reason why we want the collaboration?"

"Yes." I guess.

"Well, uh, we think we can work faster and smarter with it. I have expected outcomes on a page in this document..." Chris tries to pull it up, but I stop him.

"Okay, I get that. Who doesn't want to work faster and smarter? So what have you tried so far?" I probably sound like a dork. But at least I'm not dressed like one.

"We shopped it with some other teams. They all seem to like it, but they don't think they are the ones to own it."

"Ouch." I know this world well. I resist the incredible urge to tell Chris about a time that happened to me recently. *This is not about me. This is not about me...*

Chris and Karen are really into the conversation. They look interested and happy to talk about the work. It feels like it could be a positive experience for all of us. "Right," Chris says. "And, the people who are interested in owning it say they don't have time. They say that they can't pile any more work on top of what they already have."

"I see." What a problem for my first *go & see* questions. "I understand the reasons you shared. I don't like them, but I get it. But, what do you think is getting in the way, here?"

"I'm not sure Joel." Chris pauses. I think he is hesitating.

"I want to help you, so I'd like to know what you're thinking—"

"Well hello!" It's Lora. Crap. What the hell is she doing here? Maybe she is pissed about the report I wrote and she's hunting me down.

The three of us quietly greet her. Lora doesn't notice how the air pressure around us just tanked.

She waves a hand and smiles. "Don't stop talking just because I am here. I happened to be in a meeting on the other end of the floor when I saw you, Joel. I wanted to see what you're up to."

More awkward silence and fidgeting as we both look at her.

"Really, I'll just listen quietly." She folds her hands and rocks back and forth on her heels.

Right.

Chris looks at me, waiting for the go ahead to continue the conversation. Whatever interested, engaged looks Karen and Chris had have now turned into tight smiles. Great. They are going to think I invited Lora along. Did I just hear a phone vibrate?

"Go ahead, Chris." I try to look encouraging.

"So, uh, we think that there is a lot of interest for one of these sites at WL, but it's going to need some focus. Maybe not forever, but a collaboration team to get things up and off the ground is probably a good idea."

"Do you think—"

"Can I offer some insight on this?" Lora asks. Karen's eyes flick to me. Man, she has no idea what she's doing. I most definitely heard a phone vibrate inside Chris' backpack, under his desk.

Chris opens his mouth to answer, but Lora jumps in before the words come out. "It's an awesome idea that's already been explored." She tells us that two players, IT and corporate communications, both wanted to own the space, and a territory fight that ensued. The players went to their corners to put together more compelling stories about why one was a better owner for it than another, and then another priority pushed this work off the table.

This was good background for them, but that's where the good stopped. Lora talked about the culture here not being ready for such dramatic change, and that now might not be the best time for this effort. Then she listed a number of other things that she considered to be of much higher priority. Some of the work she mentioned I had never heard of until now. I had a strong urge to tell her she is talking over all of our heads, but I felt the moment was hopeless.

Then she nailed the coffin shut. "So, basically, it's a lot of wasted work."

Crushing words. More awkward silence, but then I felt I must speak. I feel the strong urge to defend my team and their creativity. Chris' phone vibrates again.

"Thanks for your thoughts, Lora."

"Yes, thank you for the feedback." Though he is completely deflated, Chris dutifully agrees, like we all have been socially engineered to do at WL.

I think I can ask a question here, which will help change the trajectory of this horrible moment. So much for my first *go & see*. I was worried about screwing up, not about Lora crashing it. Well, blowing it to bits.

I try to break through this if-you-only-knew-what-I-knew moment. "Wow, Lora just mentioned a lot of work. All of us have so much to do."

"We sure do," Karen agrees. I think she is sensing my effort. Why do I not work with this woman more?

"Chris, can you give me an example of how having a collaboration site like the ones you have researched could help you work smarter?"

Lora is standing there, just waiting to pounce. We can all feel it. Chris' phone vibrates again. The entire team must be texting him. I really can't blame them.

"Yeah." Chris gives an example of how the work they do sometimes requires a specific technology skill for just a short amount of time: recently, his team needed a person with a specific developer skill that they didn't have on their team. Their manager Vijay sent a request through "the system." It took three weeks to find someone in the organization who had the skill. The good news was that they found someone with the needed skills, and the bad news is that he wasn't available to help for another week because of a big project.

When the developer finally connected with them, and helped with the issue, they learned some startling news from him. Apparently, the developer did have time to help them the week before, but he first knew of the request for help yesterday.

"So what you're saying is the manager held back the request for help because they didn't want to share their resource?" Lora asks.

"Basically, yeah. But that's not the—"

"That's hoarding, and that's unacceptable." She announces as if it's a discovery. Managers have been doing it for my entire career here. Not mine, at least, I don't think they have... Never mind.

"The kicker is, the developer helped us in just two hours," Chris says. "We waited over three weeks for just two hours of niche dev time."

Lora folds her arms. "That's crazy. There is so much wrong with this situation."

I have to stop her from taking us off the rails. This is so hard. Why is this so hard?

"Chris, let's say we forget about the hoarding part of this for just a moment." I look at Lora. "It sounds like you had a very short-term need and the skills database process we have wasn't the right path for what you needed."

"Yes." He takes a breath, and looks at Lora. "With a collaboration tool, these small requests don't have to go through the formal processes, and we can get quick turnaround."

Karen joins in. "I could picture Chris putting the request on the collaboration site, maybe in a developer group. Word would travel quickly, and we could talk with someone about our needs, probably the same day."

"Exactly." Chris builds on Karen's scenario. "We might find it's a bigger deal than we thought, and have to go back to that formal skills database to hire someone. Or, we might get the help we need in a matter of hours or days, instead of weeks. It's just one of about 50 examples we've collected through our research."

I thank Chris for the example. Lora is not impressed. More phone vibrations. This must be their entertainment for the day. The team probably goes to the bar just to deal with this leadership. Once again, my eyes feel a little more open than yesterday.

"Research." She repeats with disdain. She looks at her watch. "I have to run. Joel, please send me a full report on this…this hoarding incident."

"But—" Before I can finish, she walks away. Another drive-by. And, another report.

I salvage what is left of my first *go & see*. At least, I try to, by thanking Karen and Chris for sharing their work with me.

"I'm not sure how, given what Lora said, but I plan to find a way to support your efforts, here. The story you told was very compelling."

"Thank you, Joel. I am really happy that you came here." He pauses. "I didn't mean to get anyone in trouble. I'm worried now. You have to write a report…" he trails off.

"I know you didn't. I didn't plan on Lora stopping by here and getting involved." I probably shouldn't have said that, but they need to know this was not an ambush.

"I'm sorry if this sounds nosy, but what kind of report are you going to write, Joel?" Karen asks.

I chuckle. "I'm not sure myself." Maybe one that I can wipe Lora's ass with? "Whatever I put together, it's going to be very, very short. I think we've already spent enough time on the topic."

"If you want help, we could do it together." Karen offers.

"Let's try it." This sounds like an opportunity to connect with them. "All we need is an hour. Do you have time this afternoon? Just so you're not canceling team meetings on account of this."

"Sure," Chris nods. "Should we meet in your office?"

"How about we meet somewhere here?" I think this is what I'm supposed to do. Stay out of my office, right?

At 1:00 p.m., I return to my team's floor to help write the bogus report for Lora. Chris and Karen want me to add my ideas and thoughts first.

It might sound crazy, or that I am crazy, but I can feel Eve in my head. What would she want me to do here? If I hadn't worked with Eve, I would have mostly written the report myself, and then thrown it over to Chris and Karen to finish. I would tell them what I want them to write. They'd probably spend a week polishing and perfecting it before giving it back to me. I would have forgotten about it until it reappeared. I'd change some of the things they wrote, maybe even some of the things I wrote, and then send it to Lora. She wouldn't read it for at least a week, if she reads it at all. Then, we'd probably have a meeting about it, and go over all of it page by page. If there was anything substantial in it from her perspective, Lora might write a new report for Rick, and basically just rip off all the stuff that the rest of us wrote.

All I know now is that writing this report should probably be different. The other thing I know is that I probably shouldn't tell them what to write. Chris already did the research, didn't he?

Karen and Chris want to know about what strategy to use with Lora's concern about hoarding. I'm concerned too, but I try not to show it. Chris has his laptop projecting, and we are pulling the report together in real time. It feels like the right thing to do.

I suggest that we take the high road strategy and avoid leading with negativity. Though Lora asked for a report on hoarding, we focus the report on the original purpose of the research. This way, I can support the idea through this report and still make it look like we are appeasing Lora.

Later, I can use the report for shopping the idea of a collaboration site. Meanwhile, Lora can use it for whatever her whim of the day is.

In the end, we have a nice summary of lost productivity examples in a concise report. It was truly a team effort. Although Lora will likely not even read it. And the part about her recycling it and giving it to Rick will still happen, too.

We finish the report in 40 minutes. Working together was really strange and good, all at once. I could hear enthusiasm in Chris and Karen's voices, so I think we all felt good about the way we got it done. I thank Karen and Chris, and offer my assurance that I will follow up with them.

Well. This is a very long tail to my first *go & see*.

Reflections

I still have no idea what I am doing.

Where is agile?

Lora depresses me.

Lora is a joke to my teams.

Go & Cause Trouble

It's only been four days since I met with Eve, but it feels like a lifetime. It's a frigid morning, and we are savoring the warm café and hot drinks. I am also savoring a break from WL.

"So how did your assignment go, Joel?" Eve's green eyes are full and waiting for my story.

I sigh. Where to begin?

"You look conflicted." Eve leans in a little. "Did you accomplish your assignment?"

"Yes. It felt a lot less like *go & see*, and a lot more like *Go & Cause Trouble*. I'm having a hard time deciphering what to tell you as it relates to your assignment and what is just corporate stuff that happens anyway."

Eve encourages me not to overthink it. And asks to see my reflections. She pages through my reflections, and reads some of the highlights:

"'Reflections: My leadership team doesn't understand why the three of us are getting agile coaching. My leadership team doesn't believe that they need to change.' Those are big ones. Oh, how about this one, 'I have been asleep at the wheel of my career for a very long time. It feels terrible.'" Her eyes meet mine, and give me some understanding. She goes back to my notebook and reads more.

"This is a great idea, Joel, 'Jack's fresh eyes to WL are helpful to me. I need to spend more time with him.'" She grins. "Bro shopping!"

She reads more, "Leaders are worried. I see things I have not seen before. Value is not an expectation at WL. I still have no idea what I am doing. Where is agile? Lora depresses me."

"Wow." Eve grins. "You've been busy growing."

"Yeah, I've been dying. But, I haven't said the word *resources* at all!" I laugh at myself. "I had no idea how hard this was going to be. And, I have a feeling it's not going to get easier."

"Don't worry about what's next. You've got a lot to digest right here." She slides my notebook back to me.

"Very true." I tell Eve about the whole experience of *go & see*, from my anxiety about messing up the questions, to the report we ended up writing together.

"Joel, I know you feel pretty bad about this first one, but it was a fantastic first one."

"You mean, my *worst* one?"

"Nope. I stick by my approval of a fantastic effort." Eve is smug. "What made it good is that you stuck with your intent that you were going there to learn."

"I feel like I am missing so many parts of the puzzle in what I'm changing about how I lead."

"You are. But that's okay. There is a lot to being an agile leader. You are working on building blocks. Value and *go & see* are huge building blocks for your journey."

I tell Eve how I feel like my eyes are slowly opening, and I'm seeing all kinds of madness I haven't seen before, or at least, haven't noticed in a long time. And, what I'm seeing is also stirring up all kinds of feelings about my career that I've packed away or ignored. It's uncomfortable and pretty depressing.

"All very disturbing, and all very normal when going through a good coaching program." Eve sips her matcha latte. "That's why I said you were doing some good growing."

"You read my reflections. What about the pushback from Lora and WL on this kind of leadership?"

Eve is giggling. I haven't heard her do that before. It might be cute, if it wasn't directed at me.

"What?"

"Pushback." She rolls her eyes. "I can't stand that word."

"It just means to disagree."

"Joel, it's a lot of things." Eve says flatly. "And…we're back to respect."

"So, am I going to have to stop using that word, too?"

"It's not nearly as bad as calling people *resources*. So you have that going for you." Eve warms her hands on her cup. "Speaking directly is respectful. If you disagree, say you disagree. If you don't like something, say you don't like it. If you think it's a bad idea because of X risk, or Y dependency, then say that. For Heaven's sake, don't say *pushback*."

So, it's way more than just a word. *Pushback* represents culture. Just like *resources*. Funny how just one word can do it. At WL, we don't speak directly about much of anything, especially disagreeing with someone. Well, except for Lora, who always speaks exactly what's on her mind. Maybe that is the one thing she does right.

"It's not just you. Somehow, WL got away from honesty, Joel."

"I'm starting to see that. You are helping me open my eyes."

"Yes," She sighs. "We have so many different places to go with this session. What is the most valuable use of our time together today?"

"You're asking *me*?"

"This is yours to build."

"True. Then we need to talk more about the fact that the leadership team above me is definitely not on board with me changing the way I lead."

"Sure. Why do you think it matters that they don't want to change?"

"Look what's happened so far when I make changes to how I lead, even small ones. The effects ripple through my leadership team, above me and below me."

Eve's not impressed with my worry. "That is the plan. You didn't think it would be welcomed with open arms, did you?"

"No, but right now the leaders above me are looking at me like a wingnut or a rebel."

"You are a rebel." Eve raises her matcha as a toast. "When you learn agile, then you will be a wingnut."

"You know what I mean, Eve. Lora hired you to help me make changes to how I lead. The changes I'm making are supposed to be good for the organization, not just me."

Eve shrugs. "They don't want to change, and so they won't like what you are doing."

"My first *go & see* story is a perfect example," I sigh.

"Yes it is."

She gets what I'm saying but she's not seeing anything wrong with it.

"You didn't think you were going to have to risk anything but your pride to do this coaching. You thought that because it was pushed down upon you, there was understanding and acceptance."

"How naïve of me."

Eve assures me that I had a natural expectation, and that I should feel validated that I wanted my leaders to act like leaders. She admits that the leaders' behavior is a huge red flag for a coach or consultant. When the top doesn't understand that they too will have to change until later in the game, change is going to be very difficult. But my revelation wasn't news to her. From the brief interactions they had to set up coaching for me, Meryll, and Jack, she was aware that Lora probably had no idea what she was getting into.

Great. I ask Eve if she's got one foot out the door. She says no, that she's having too much fun helping me change. As charming of a response that is, I hope it's true. It's been the most uncomfortable, but great experience I've ever had.

She circles back on the idea that I should be doing this for *me*, not for Lora or anyone else. First and foremost, I need to be a good leader no matter where I work.

"Your mind has been startled out of a very long sleep and wants to do something about the discomfort…right now. Because being uncomfortable is not what we humans like. But don't be fooled into this thinking. You don't need to do anything right now, but focus on growth and learning, two very uncomfortable things. See where I'm going?"

"Yes."

"You can remain in this transition state for some time, and not have to do anything but keep working on you. It's a really uncomfortable place to be, but it's not as unsafe as you think. You are learning tons, and transforming into a great leader."

I'm out of coffee and ideas. "I can leave any time I like, right?"

Eve gives me a thumbs up. "Exactly. So, you don't have to choose Lora over coaching, or coaching over Lora. You haven't had to think like this for a very long time—"

"Ever!"

"Somehow, you or the culture at WL got you thinking that you are in a marriage. You know, that you are together no matter the weather."

I sigh. I want to throw up. And at the same time, I want to laugh with the excitement I feel about anything being possible. I could be free of Lora if I wanted to be. I'm not trapped here at all. God, I really was asleep.

"You look pale." Eve peers at me. "What are you thinking?"

"I'm thinking that I am going to be sick."

"I thought so." Green eyes soften. "I'm sorry you have to go through this rite of passage."

I challenge Eve on that one. Of course she has an answer. Apparently, most leaders who go through this intense coaching experience, and honestly work on changing, have incredible lows. She calls it being stripped down to the core to be built back up. Sounds like boot camp, without all the yelling. Without Lora.

We pause and rest for a moment. I'm still frustrated with how much time I've wasted. "Life moves fast. Before you know it, five years have passed…" I think of how 20 years whizzed by, mostly without me looking. "I lost my two feet rule mindset."

"Yep. I assure you, it's normal. Depressing, but normal." She folds her café napkin into a tiny Chinese fan. "But stop thinking about whether you should feel this way or that way, or if Lora and Rick should be doing this or that. It's only going to drive you mad."

"Focus on me." I say it but I'm not sure I mean it yet.

"Right. Focus on your challenges. I'm here to help, but we only get to focus together a few hours a week. The job is mostly on your shoulders."

"It's sort of what I did when I was working with Karen and Chris, and then Lora showed up. You were totally in my head."

Eve grins. "That is exactly what happened. See? It didn't feel great, but it was the right thing to do. The part about being a leader, not the part about me being in your head."

"Right." I roll my eyes. "Seriously, just seeing Chris and Karen being so into their idea, and hearing the enthusiasm in their voices told me we were on the right track. It felt good, too."

Eve shares that unwinding a command and control leader mindset is going to take time. Yeah, that's me, Mr. Command and Control. It's so disturbing to think of myself this way, especially because most of the time, I don't know I'm doing it. Everyone around me is leading the same way, and our environment is set up for it, so how would I? No wonder trying to change makes me feel like a wingnut or rebel. It's against the grain of everything and everyone around me.

Eve says that as my coach, she is strategically selecting the changes she wants me to make, and in the order I make them. From the beginning, I believed there was a method to her madness. Until now, I didn't think we'd ever get to the stuff about agile leader coaching. What I'm learning is that I am living it right now. Every building block she gives me is going to help me release my command and control leadership style, in favor of agile leadership. Eve made it very clear that, first and foremost agile leaders are simply good leaders. That is the part we are working on right now.

Today Eve showed me that I don't need to report to a good leader to be one. I need to accept the fact that I won't ever have perfect conditions in which to grow. Instead of looking at Lora or Rick for answers, I need to just start with me. Easy to say, hard to do.

We are at the end of our meeting, so it's time for a breakthrough project. Eve comments on the huge accomplishment I had this week, and how awesome it was. Because of this big leap, we're not piling on another big assignment.

"Joel, I was going to assign you to take Chris' idea forward to your director team, but it sounds like you are already doing that."

"Yes. I had no reason to wait."

"Great." She says. "We're going to keep working on *value*. As a leader, you want to deliver value to your customers as quickly as possible."

"All righty. Sounds fair." Now what?

"This week, when you *go & see*, keep asking your three questions. That will never change, so keep practicing. Hopefully, you'll get more chances to do that without Lora around. And for a lighter assignment, ask your teams: *who is your customer?* You can do it on your walk, or if you visit a team meeting, you can ask them there. Make notes in your wonderful notebook."

"Got it."

I leave J&L's café feeling better than when I arrived. My situation hasn't changed, but my outlook has. I'll take that as a win. As for this next assignment, I have a really simple question to ask my teams. It shouldn't be that hard. At least, that's what I thought the last time I had a simple assignment.

Francie Van Wirkus

Reflections

Simple questions are rarely simple.

My growth is not dependent on my leader's growth.

I can be a good leader and report to a bad leader.

Where is agile?

Ask a Simple Question

Armed with my new breakthrough project, I decide to try it out first on my two amigos, Meryll and Jack. When I asked them the question, they just looked at me. There is my first indication that this is not going to be a simple assignment.

"Did you answer this question for yourself?" Jack asks.

"Yeah. I thought about it on the drive home last night. If I tell you what I think, I won't get your honest answer."

"This is dumb," Meryll grouses. "Everyone here knows our customer is the end user out there in the world."

I can tell Jack likes the question. He's no longer slouching. "Yeah, well what about the people who sell our products to these end users?"

Meryll looks at me. "You said *end* customer, didn't you?"

"No. Just...*who is your customer?*"

"So, it could be our sales force," Jack says.

"I guess it's them, too." Meryll hesitates.

Jack keeps pushing. "And what about the business and tech people at WL who support those people who sell the stuff to the end users?"

"Why would *they* count as customers?" Meryll asks. "They aren't using the final product."

"No, but without them, our sales force couldn't sell our final product. No training, no tech support, no marketing data or programs."

"Well, then, I guess they are our customers, too."

"Then there are tech people who support the apps that our sales people use."

Meryll's had enough. "Fine. They are our customers too. Don't forget the toilet paper company we all use." She rolls her eyes. "Come on, Joel. This is not that hard. Everyone knows we have an end user."

"Right. But you both had a big hesitation when I first asked the question. I did too. Because when I heard the question, a lot of different ideas popped into my head."

"Is there one customer more important than the other?"

"Different question Jack," I say. "I can't even go there yet because I'm still working on my customers."

"That's a great question to ask your teams, Joel. I wonder if they have a better handle on it than we do."

"I wouldn't be surprised," Meryll sighs. It seems like she is sliding down into the depressive place I'm at. I wish I could help her, but I'm there, too.

"I'm going to talk with my coach about it."

"Me too," Meryll chimes in. "Your coach sounds cool, Joel. Mine is just sort of okay."

"It's not a competition," I say flatly. "Please don't start thinking it is. We are all in this together, each taking our own journeys with our own coach."

It's obvious they are not as deep into things as me. I sure don't want this to turn into a *haves and have nots* thing. I encourage them to give their coaches, and more importantly the process, a chance. I have no idea what I'm doing, but it sure feels better than the miserable path I was on.

I remind my colleagues that I didn't like Eve much when we started working together, mostly because of what she represented: forced change. Not knowing her, I had no reason to like or dislike her. Now having worked with her for a few weeks, she has earned my respect and trust. It's shaky ground, but good enough for me to keep doing the challenging breakthroughs she asks of me. She hasn't steered me wrong yet. Even if she does, I'm not sure I can get too hung up about *her*. She is one person up against huge change. Can she really take on the huge gap between WL culture and me being a good leader?

That afternoon, I take my question to my teams. I begin again with the familiar: Vijay's team. This time, I stop at Vijay's desk and ask him if he wants to join me. His eyes light up and he joins me. I tell him I'm not very good yet, but I think it's important for him to see what I'm doing, even when I'm messing it up. Vijay wants to know the question I'm going to ask, but I tell him to watch me ask it of his team first. If I ask him the question now, his brain will start churning, and then he won't be able to focus on *go & see*.

Karen's not at her desk, so we keep walking and find her at Chris' desk.

"You're back," Karen smiles. "And you have an intern." She nods at Vijay.

Vijay owns his role and smiles, "That's right. But don't worry, I'm just along for the ride to observe." I just know he'll do a better job of observing than Lora did.

I tee up my question by telling them I'm not testing or quizzing them, but I'm here to learn. I want to know things from their perspective. I offer that it might be sort of odd to have your director and manager asking the question, but try to think of us as wanting to learn from you. Then I ask the question.

Both Karen and Chris respond at the same time, "Our end users."

I nod my head to let them know I heard them, but I say nothing. I'm trying to be as neutral as possible, and it's really hard. I'm waiting for them to really start thinking about it, like Meryll and Jack did.

Vijay is uncomfortable in the silence. "Is that correct?" he asks.

"It's not about it being correct. It's about the discussion." I say, "So your customer is the end user. No others?"

"Well, we have lots of customers," Karen offers.

"Yeah," Chris agrees. "But when you, as a leader, ask the question, I think of our end customer. If Karen asked me who our customer is, I might say it's another team that we support."

"Yeah, we have tons of types of customers and tons of customers."

I thank them and move on to others in the area, and ask them the same question. Vijay is eagerly observing and appears to love every moment. Interesting that most people on the floor answered without hesitation, that our customer is our end user.

I took my notes and visited my other teams to ask the same question. I didn't walk with the managers there, as I haven't talked through my changes in leadership as much with them as with Vijay. I have every intention to, but the time isn't right. I have more work to do on me first. Besides, most of these managers were not at their desks when I visited their area. I was told they were in one-on-one meetings with other team members.

My research got more interesting over time. I found that the more people I asked, the more diverse the answers were. I even ran into a few pockets of disagreement among team members like Meryll and Jack did. Also, the teams wanted to know what I was going to do with my research. I told them I was working on the word *value*, and that understanding who our customer is helps me understand value. Other than that, I'm going to take my findings back to my coach, and talk about what's next with her.

Reflections

I haven't given my customer much thought.

Everyone I have talked to thinks we have different customers.

A Full Report

I'm on my way to a one-on-one with Rick when Lora stops me in the hall. "Do you have time right now?"

I apologize and tell her I'm meeting with Rick for the next hour, and I'm booked the rest of the day. I know where this exchange is going to go. I'm going to get a huge hammer pounded on me for trying to change. This is exactly what Eve and I talked about yesterday.

"How about at 5:00?" She's full of urgency. "Do you have time then?"

"I don't have time at 5:00. What's up? Can we talk tomorrow? I have time tomorrow." I'm trying to stay calm, knowing full well she is going to crash my time with Rick.

"I want to talk with you about the report on your meetings attendance. What are you doing at 5:00?"

"Driving home, Lora." *This is not an emergency. Don't cave in! I must stick to my guns.* A meeting about my calendar report is not an emergency. Now I'm pissed. Old Joel would have rolled over and met her at 5:00. New Joel will not take the bait.

"Oh." Lora really doesn't like my answer. "I'm out of the office all day tomorrow. I will crash your one-on-one with Rick. He should get involved in this anyway. See you in a few minutes." Lora walks away quickly. Probably has to go get her hammer from her office...

"Sit down, Joel." Rick encourages me into his office, where Lora is already waiting. "Lora wanted to join us, so I let her crash. She's got some questions about a report you wrote."

For the next 20 minutes, Lora grills me about my commitment, with Rick passively watching. Through it all, I stand firm on one word: value. Man, I have no idea what I am doing, but I understand the definition of value. Choosing my words carefully, I tell them what I've learned from my coach: I'm either adding value or taking away from it.

"Joel has this crazy idea about being home at 5:30 p.m. every night," Lora accuses.

Rick raises his eyebrows. "Sounds good to me."

Lora rolls her eyes.

"Tell me more about your strategy, Joel. Maybe I can look at where I am—"

"Don't you see what's happening here, Rick?" Lora interrupts. "I'm just going to come right out and say it: he's avoiding work."

Rick and Lora have an exchange as if I'm not even there. Would Eve want me to interject and stand up for myself? I think she'd want me to observe, and see where they land. So I keep my mouth shut while Lora flaps hers. The pressure in the room increases with each word she speaks.

"Lora," Rick holds up his hand, "Let's let Joel try what his coach is suggesting. After all, we did hire the coaches."

"This isn't going to work. I can't always replace Joel in these meetings—"

"You don't need to replace him." Rick sat back in his chair. He's relaxing, which is a good sign. "In fact, do not try to insert yourself where he has pulled out. That's not going to test anything."

"The user experience meeting can't be avoided like that—"

Rick's voice is firm. "Since Joel has the communication lines open with the owners of these meetings, I'm not at all worried about him avoiding anything."

"But—"

"They know they can pull him in when they need him."

Lora's wrath has been neutralized for now. She stands to leave, and then reaches for my report.

Rick holds his hand out to stop her from taking it. "I'm going to keep this, Lora. I want to learn more about how to get home at 5:30 p.m., even if it's only one day a week." He smiles at me, "I hope you don't mind."

My words were a little slow to come out. "Not at all."

"Fine." Lora fakes a smile. "I'd love to hear what you learn, Rick." Lora's failing miserably at backpedaling on her witch hunt. She's not leaving his office yet, but he clearly wants her to go. Rick offers her a cordial thank you, and then she leaves. The room pressure lightens immediately.

Rick puts my report aside, and then folds his hands on his desk and smiles at me. "What's new?"

Well this is awkward.

We have an interesting conversation about some research that was done about collaboration at WL. Rick asks me if there is any summary on it. I tell him Karen and Chris wrote a report with my help, and that we gave it to Lora last week. Rick's face twitched ever so slightly of FOMO before he asked me for a copy of it. I was happy to oblige, sending it from my laptop. As I hit the Send button, I know this action is going to set off a chain reaction in my surrounding world. All because of one word.

Reflections

I am making change in me and how I lead my teams.

When I am with my teams, it feels good to make change.

When I am with Lora, it feels terrible to make change.

I found opportunity to change without Eve telling me to do it. Coaching must be working!

Ohno's Circle

Arriving at J&L's café, Eve catches me before I order my coffee. "We're going to do something a little different today, Joel. Order your coffee, and then we'll meet with Lilly, one of the café managers."

"All righty." Why was I expecting to just get coffee and then sit down?

After we both have our drinks, we meet the manager in her tiny office in back. It's clear Eve and Lilly have already met, and they know something I don't know.

Eve turns to me, "Joel, we're doing some hands on learning today. Lilly is gracious enough to offer her café to us for practice. We're going to begin in the front of the café where the customers are served, then move to the supply area, and then go back out to the front."

"Got it." I smile at both of them.

"Just relax," Eve smiles. "This is going to be fun. And when we're finished, we're going to share our findings with Lilly."

"Take your coats off, and please make yourselves comfortable," Lilly smiles. "I can't wait to hear what you find."

Right, make myself comfortable. I'm so far from comfort I can barely speak.

Eve and I walk out to the busy café. She pulls a piece of chalk out of her pocket. She walks over to the part of the coffee bar where people pick up their drinks and steps back about five feet. Not many people notice her because they are all focused on getting their caffeine. Then, using the chalk, she draws a circle the size of a large beach ball on the chic, slate floor. She motions for me to come over by her.

"You have your notebook and pen?" She asks.

"Right here."

"Here's what you need to do…" Eve assigns me the task of standing in the circle, facing all the action of the ordering, making and pick up of J&L's drinks. I am to look for waste and write what I see in my notebook. She says it doesn't matter that neither of us are café business experts to do this. I offer a weak protest that we haven't studied waste much. Eve counters with how we have studied value, and by doing that, I have enough knowledge to know the opposite of it.

"So, waste in how the work is being done?" I'm still not sure about this assignment.

"*Any* waste. Don't think too hard about it. Just watch."

"All righty."

"Trust me," She smiles, walking over to a nearby café table.

"I do. That is what scares me."

I stand in the circle, braving a few curious stares of the caffeine-starved customers who are waiting for their drink to be made. I'm looking for waste, the opposite of value. I am here to learn. I don't care what others think of what I'm doing here. Oh, hey, maybe they think I am a quality jerk from the café's home office. Great. I guess I do care what they think of me.

I watch the baristas and the movement of the customers. Five minutes pass very slowly. I'm not getting this assignment. It all seems to be in good order. After ten minutes, I write a few things in my notebook just so I look like I have a purpose in my chalk circle. I couldn't find any waste. They run a pretty tight ship. After a painful 20 minutes, Eve relieves me from my post, and we go back to Lilly's office.

"What did you find, Joel? What did you write down?" Eve tries to lean over and read my notebook, upside down.

"Uh, I really didn't see anything that was out of whack." I know this is the wrong answer, but I got nothing. "I couldn't find any waste."

Eve doesn't look surprised. "All right. Everything is fine out there. Nothing can be improved."

"Not that I could see."

Eve teaches me that a big part of *go & see,* and the questions I ask there, are to help continually improve the flow of work, so teams can more efficiently and effectively produce higher quality and greater value for the customers. That's a mouthful, so she breaks it down for me: by going to see the people closest to the work, and observe their work while asking specific questions, I can help find waste.

Eve gives me the history of Ohno's Circle, named after Taiichi Ohno. I bristle, going to that quality jerk label, but she pushes past it. An industrial engineer and businessman, Ohno later became an executive vice president at Toyota. Ohno invented a new way of making improvements at Toyota. He went to where the work was being done, used chalk to draw a circle on the floor, and stood inside it. While standing in that circle for hours, he would watch and think about what he was seeing. What was getting in the way of people creating value? What situation was causing this? He would use his observations to get a look into how to make lasting improvements. Ohno then trained each of his managers to do the same. One by one, they stood in the circle for hours and learned to see their world with a new lens.

Ohno made the manager stand on the floor for *hours*? Wow. "So, are you going to make me stand in the café all day?" I'm only slightly worried.

"No. We are going to modify it so you can get back to work."

Eve takes me to the supply room of the café. It smells wonderful, and is full of coffee beans, paper products, and other café supplies. The doors to the cooler are right there, too. That must be where they keep the milk and other drinks. She makes a circle out of masking tape on the floor and asks me to stand in it.

"Let's try it again in this storage room. I'd make you stand in the cooler, but I think you might rebel."

I just sigh. This woman…this coaching…

She takes my sigh as agreement. "The team members should be coming in soon to restock, so watch closely. They've been told to go about their usual business and not change a thing."

I'm back in my circle. Eve is hanging out in Lilly's office.

"This all comes back to agile, right?" I call to her from my post.

"You bet!" She calls back. "Agile hates waste just as much as lean."

"What's agile about standing in one place?"

"Customer value!" She calls back.

She has an answer for everything.

It's easier to be here without customers nearby. I look around at the storage shelves and all of the different products on them. There is a nice, rolling step ladder to use for getting stuff on the high shelves. Just then a team member walks in and over to the napkins. He pulls out the box, opens it, and takes two armfuls of napkin bundles. As he is walking out, another team member is walking in. Even though there is not a door, the worker walking in had no idea the other worker was about to enter the storage room. They nearly collide, but neither seems alarmed about it. It must happen often, because there was no *excuse me, sorry,* or any of that. Huh. I make a note.

I make several more notes as time passes in my circle. Thirty minutes pass faster than the 20 out in the store front.

"Let's look at what you found." Eve and I put my notebook on Lilly's desk.

Looking for Waste @ J&L's Café

Workers nearly bump into each other when entering and exiting the room. Seems like a hazard. Is that waste? It could make waste.

Workers have to move a box of one product to access the actual product they need.

Several trips of hand carry to refill gallons of milk.

One short team member had to keep adjusting her apron. It's way too big for her.

"Great work, Joel."

"You're impressed?" I wasn't.

"You found more than last time. Later, we'll share all of this with Lilly. All right, now that you have some context, let's go back out to the café floor and try it again. Let's try 30 minutes this time."

I'm back in my spot, but this time I see all kinds of things that look like waste. For example, a napkin holder that's stuffed so full of napkins, that when a customer tries to pull one out, he rips five or six of them before pulling out one that can actually be used. The honey packets are so small and hard to open, that more packets are taken than needed, and much of it is wasted because it drips out during the struggle to open them.

I'm busy writing when I'm suddenly interrupted. "What the hell are you doing?"

I look up to see Meryll standing in front of me. Great.

The only way to go with this scene is to act as if everything I'm doing is completely normal. "What does it look like I'm doing?" I'm very official. Certifiable, even. "I'm looking for waste."

"You're looking for waste," Meryll says flatly. "Wow." She leans over to try and read my notebook; I pull it away so she can't read it.

Maybe I can distract her. "Did you order a medium marshmallow crème chai?"

"No. I never come here. They don't do it right, but I'm in a jam today." Meryll is still taking in the whole scene. It's driving her mad and giving me great joy. I look over at Eve, who winks at me. She doesn't have to know Meryll to know what's going on, here.

"Seriously, Joel. What are you doing?"

"I am looking for waste. I have ten minutes left." I try to look around where she is standing. Then, brilliance strikes. I simply write down Meryll.

"Hey, did you just write my name?" She can't stand it. She tries to grab my notebook.

I pull it away.

"You could do a better job hiding your notebook if you had a suit jacket on. Oh, wait! That's right. This is New Mr. GQ Joel. You know, the one that stands in a circle in the local café looking like a total dork."

You know what's next. She's going to ask about Eve.

Meryll scans the café. "So where is Eve? No way would you do this without her making you." Her eyes meet Eve's, and Eve smiles slightly and waves.

"*That's* your coach?" Meryll growls under her breath. "She is smokin' hot."

I'm busy writing. "Whatever, Meryll. She has me so uncomfortable, I can't see straight. I couldn't—"

"Stop!" Meryll holds up a hand. "I can't take another word. This is totally unfair. I have Randy, aka Melvin Milktoast, and you have...Eve, goddess of everything."

"She races Ironman triathlons, too." I add.

She rolls her eyes. "Sickening."

"Are you finished? Because I have a waste assignment I'm trying to complete." I refuse to lose my focus on my task. I think I just saw a barista reach over another barista. Huh.

"Good thing my drink is ready. See you later Joel." Meryll gives Eve one more glance, and then picks up her drink and walks out of the café.

When my time in the circle is up, Eve and I regroup one last time in Lilly's office.

"So, was that Meryll?"

"How did you know?"

"Just a guess. She seemed pretty wound up about something, which reminded me of your stories about her." I show her my list. We have all sorts of things to talk about. Very interesting how I missed so much the first time.

"Look what happens when you focus, when there is nothing more important to do."

"I get that. Things you are blind to each day become visible. It's like mushroom picking," I shrug.

"Mushroom picking?"

"Yeah." I enjoy explaining a concept to Eve, for a change. "Once you find some, you start seeing more and more. You get this lens that you didn't have before."

Eve grins. "I love it. That's exactly the point of this exercise, Joel."

"So, when I *go & see*, I should be looking at the team's gemba for waste."

"Right. And, where is the team's gemba?"

"In their head, and in their meetings and interactions."

"Right! So then, how would you look for waste in a knowledge worker's gemba?"

"Uh, ask the three questions?"

"That's right." Eve affirms. "The questions respect your team and their work. *Go & see* is all about understanding reality before acting. This is a lean leader concept. And an agile concept, which is based on empiricism."

Huh.

"So, you built this for me over many weeks: going to the place where value is added, asking key questions about what's being done, and looking for waste. What about the *who is my customer* question? Where does that fit in?"

"This was built with intention. But don't mistake intent for being linear. Your agile leader journey is a rustic road, with lots of twists and turns. I will ask you to keep trusting me, even when you get really uncomfortable." Eve is full of intensity. "And, we are not finished. There is so much more. But feel great about what we have connected so far. You've made great progress."

"So…"

"We'll talk about who is your customer every time we meet. I won't lose track of it. You've got notes on it, which is great. We can use those in the future."

We rest for a moment.

"Okay. I see the connections, but I don't feel them yet. Does that make sense?"

"Don't worry about it. You are right on track. A curvy, undulating track." Eve pushes my notebook back to me. "Don't worry. You won't become a quality jerk."

"I'll come find you." I point at her.

"You know, we could really geek out on lean and talk about the different kinds of waste we saw, but we're going to stick to high level. I find most IT leaders and staff love to get really wrapped up in naming and differentiating things like this. Resist the temptation to look like the smartest person in the room, and just look for waste."

"Got it. I think."

"You're probably wondering if I'm going to assign you to stand in a circle in your teams' areas."

"Yeah."

"Not happening. Bake this experience into your three questions when you visit your teams."

"For once, I think I can do the breakthrough."

Eve looks disappointed. "Maybe we didn't make this one hard enough."

"Standing in a chalk circle, in a busy café? Yeah, I think you made it hard enough."

After work, I pull into the garage and get out of my car. Something stops me. Every night, I get out of my car and have to twist sideways to avoid brushing against that damn shelving unit with Cele's gardening stuff on it. It's been that way since we moved into this house a little over a year ago. Just because. I look at the rest of the things along the garage wall, and see space that could be made open if I move a few things. Lower profile things that won't get near the driver's side car doors.

I put my gym backpack and laptop bag down, and switch the bulky shelving unit for the lower profile stuff. I step back and admire my work. Problem solved. Huh. That effort took me about two minutes. I've been coping for over a year, because I didn't see it.

The next morning, it happens again, this time in the locker room at the pool. I've just showered after a quick 3,000m swim. I open my locker and dig in the back for my deodorant. There is an empty one in my way. Why is that in there? There is an Axe Anarchy deodorant that my son Elliot lent me when I was in a jam last week. I never returned that smelly crap to him. There is an old swimming cap that I never wear anymore, but it's from the first triathlon I ever did. I move that thing around every time I'm in here. Ah, found the deodorant. The right one.

So now I'm seeing waste in two ways: first, I have to move stuff out of the way to get what I'm really after. And holding onto stuff that I'm not using. That is not adding value. The swim cap is looking a little moldy. I never noticed that before. If that cap had so much value, I should have put it up on the wall in the basement by the kid's awards and trophies. Now it's junk. I throw out the cap and the empty deodorant, and throw Elliot's Axe in my backpack. He can have it back. I cringe picturing him going to school smelling like that. Then again, maybe it's good he is wearing it; might make fine girl repellant.

Right then and there, I decide to attack my locker. It took about four minutes to pull everything out and then reorganize it. Other than the moldy cap, I'm not really a slob. I just…don't take time to make it better.

Driving to work, it hits me again. I've been asleep. Eve's coaching has disrupted me in ways I never imagined, and she says we're just beginning. Before the Ohno's circle exercise, I thought I was fully awake and alert to what I needed to change. Not that I knew what all of it meant. This awakening has hit me from all angles.

Now I know there is more. Lots more. Doesn't matter what it is right now, just that it's out there. Doesn't matter if I don't believe I can handle any more change, either. Eve is a master at helping me find more inside...*me*. All I have to do is be willing to see it.

Reflections

I think I am a good leader, but I am not.

Once again, I have been asleep.

Waste is everywhere. Where is value?

Powerful Presence

"So, Eve is hot, eh?"

"Grow up, Jack." Meryll huffs.

Of course Meryll told Jack. She couldn't stand keeping such information to herself. "I am so busy being uncomfortable, I barely notice."

I stand up and look out my window. When I turn around and look at my credenza, I see an old WL employee benefits brochure. I think it's old. Picking it up, I can see it's from two years ago. I throw it in my recycle bin. Finding waste is happening all of the time now.

Jack smirks and rolls his eyes. "Riiight, Joel." He points at my recycle bin. "What are you doing anyway?"

"What? It's a benefits brochure from two years ago. I don't need it anymore, so out it goes."

Jack and Eve look at each other and giggle like first graders.

"Ever since she made him stand in that circle, he's been finding all kinds of waste." Jack clasps his hands together under his chin. "Oooh."

"She's like, a model," Meryll adds. "How can she possibly be good at coaching?"

"She's got him doing cool stuff like standing in a circle to look for waste." Jack reasons. "My coach Frank doesn't have me do anything cool. I'm just reading boring books."

"You're reading books?"

"Yeah. We've only met in person once. Each week I'm assigned to read a chapter in like, four different books. Then, we have a phone conference once a week to talk about them."

"That's weird, Jack." Meryll wrinkles her nose.

Jack shrugged. "I thought that's just what we all do for the first month or so."

Meryll looks at me. "Are these coaches from the same firm?"

I shrug. "I'm not sure it matters."

Meryll is concerned. "Well, I've only met with my coach Randy two times, but he hasn't assigned any books for me to read. We should ask our coaches."

"Sure. But…why?"

"So Jack can get a different one, moron. He can't fall behind us. You're already sprinting ahead."

"Hmmm." Meryll had a great point, from an angle Jack and I never considered. Just because we have to do agile leader coaching, doesn't mean we have to keep the coach we have. Just when I think Meryll is completely beaten down, she throws us a fastball. One of the many reasons I like working with her.

"Thanks Meryll." Jack says. "Books are okay, but that's not coaching. The stuff you're talking about with Melvin Milktoast, and the stuff The Hottie is making Joel do sounds like real coaching."

We strategize about how to tell Lora.

"Wait a second." I hold up my hand. "I don't think we need to ask Lora."

"You're right, Joel." Jack says. "I can just call her and tell her I want a different coach. I'll ask to speak to their match maker, or whatever they call the person. Lora doesn't need to get involved."

"Make sure you tell her you want a hottie," Meryll adds.

I can't stand it. "Look, I'm sure when Lora hired the coaching firm she didn't say, '*Be sure and give Joel the hot one, and Meryll and Jack can have the geeks.*'"

Jack sighs. "Hard to imagine who Lora might think is hot, male or female…"

"Eew," Meryll squirms. "Just imagining her, you know—"

"Stop!" Jack holds up his hand. "I can't take any more."

"We have to find a way to get Lora out of our heads. She's not that powerful. We are not going to change into agile leaders with her and Rick in our heads."

"Oh really?" Meryll chuckles. "Is this another learning from The Hottie?"

Jack laughs. "I'll do whatever you say, Eve." He whines, "You want me to stand in a circle for a few hours? Of course I will. Your wish is my command. By the way, can I rub your feet—"

I jerk my thumb toward the door. "I'm going to kick you two out if you don't stop."

"Oooh. Joel's defending his hottie." Meryll can't help herself. I think I see something, so I call her on it.

"You know, Meryll, Lora doesn't have as much power as we give her. That makes you squirm, doesn't it?"

"She *is* that powerful, Joel. She can fire you, remember? When did you get so brave? Or have you completely lost it?" Meryll throws up her hands.

"Yes, she can fire me, but she is way too deep in our heads. Every move I make here shouldn't be clouded by her control. I don't know what to do about it because I'm first noticing it."

Jack catches up with my thoughts. "Seeing it is a first step. A painful, uncomfortable first step."

Meryll stands up. "I don't know why you both have started using the word *uncomfortable* so much. It's not like we're supposed to be comfortable at work."

"Meryll, hear me out," I plead. Yes, plead. I need Meryll, really need her to come with us. We have this incredibly difficult journey upon us. Jack will be fine with it, but Meryll, she is more fragile. She has been so much more affected by Lora. Like me, I believe Meryll can be a great leader, if she can get past Lora's wrath. And a little agile coaching. But without Meryll, our journey will be so much more difficult.

"Lora's bad leadership has infiltrated our lives, every hour of every day at WL. We are listing so far toward her, we are nearly paralyzed…in what we think and in what we do." I lower my voice. "We can't get rid of her, but we can right the ship."

"What if you right the ship and lose your job?" Meryll leans against the window, and looks at the mountains in the distance. They look so peaceful compared to the mood in this room.

"All I ask is that you think about it, Meryll." I tell her she's an incredibly talented woman who deserves to grow with the best, not be beaten down by a commander. I challenge her to think if her regular WL paycheck under the tyranny of Lora (and Rick, for that matter) is better than looking for a new job. There are tons of jobs out there. This isn't 2009, with things tanking all around us.

Jack says that even if it were 2009, and jobs were scarce, he would be looking. He said no amount of job security is worth having a leader climb up your ass and into your head the way Lora does. Not the most pleasant analogy, but he's right on. The truth.

We end the discussion with Meryll, once again, having to think it over. I was encouraged when she said she's going to bring it to her coach. Now that they've met a few times, she wants to get more out of it. Actually, I'm surprised she hasn't gotten something out of it already. Maybe Melvin Milktoast is no match for battling WL culture? I guess I assumed that we all had strong coaches. Maybe not.

Reflections

I give Lora too much power.

Jack, Meryll and I give Lora too much power.

I'm leading a change that I don't understand yet.

Jack's coach stinks.

True Confessions

The next morning Meryll stops in my office. She asks if I have time to talk. Of course I do. She closes the door and sits down. At least she's not pacing the floor out of the gate. I anticipate our conversation: lots of gloom and doom and worry about me bucking the system, and that it's not worth it to push Lora. Notice I didn't say *"give Lora pushback."* I'm really trying!

Meryll looks haggard at best. She's usually so put together, it really strikes me. "You look tired, Meryll." I study her concerned face. "Everything okay?" It's clearly not.

"I've been thinking about this whole awakening you've had. And you know, you're waking me up, too. This coaching thing is the most incredible experience I've had in a long, long while." She smiles but her eyes are tearing up. "It's just…you're showing me things that scare me."

I sit down in the guest chair next to Meryll. Although I'm afraid to know, I ask her what scares her. She tells me that when her coach and I started opening her eyes, it has set off a chain reaction of stuff in her personal life. Stuff that's been ready to boil over, and now it has. I knew she and her husband Al have been separated for a while, but I thought things were stable. They are not.

I think back to the times Jack and I tried to cheer her up. She always downplayed her situation, saying that being at work as an escape from her problems. She never wanted to talk about her separation, so we never did.

And Cele and I were just on Meryll and Al's boat last summer. That big, amazing boat…

She filed for a divorce last week. Al is in rehab for a gambling problem, and their house is in foreclosure. Al spent every dime they had saved. Meryll and their two kids have to move out by the end of the month. She's found a towne home close to school, but she's devastated that they lost their house.

My heart sank for Meryll. And Al. And the kids. This is so horribly huge. No wonder she's been so wound up lately. No wonder she is scared to do anything new. From the sound of it, it's a miracle she's even making it to work every day.

"You want to be bold at work, and I just want to…curl up and stay where I am. But I know that where I am is a farce, too." Meryll's crying. "My job and my marriage have been a big lie."

Do I hug her? Yes. She is my friend, and she is falling to pieces right before my eyes. If not me, then who?

"I'm sorry." Meryll realizes she is crying on my shirt, and pulls away.

"Don't worry about it, Meryll. You're my friend, and I care. This is a massive thing; you can't expect to hold it all up on your own."

"The only thing real is that I'm a mother to two children."

"No, you're an awesome mother to two children, Meryll. They are great kids. And you are a great Mom. No one can change that." Meryll is a mess and needs my friendship. But I sure hope I don't say anything dumb to make it worse.

"All these years I've been frozen. All this time I thought I was building a great career." Meryll wipes her tears with a tissue from my desk. "It's like Lora has held us back from growing as leaders."

"She has. Rick has too. The way he leads Lora has a lot to do with the way she leads *us*." I offer her another tissue. "And we let this happen to us. It was a two-way street, but we didn't know it."

"God, I'm so blind." She holds her head in her hands and sobs. "I'm so dumb."

"No, you trusted your husband like married people are supposed to. And, we trusted Lora like we were supposed to. But then we fell asleep at the wheel of our own careers. That doesn't mean we are dumb or bad. We weren't looking at the right things."

She picks her head up. "Well our coaches are sure as hell changing that!" There is a spark in her eyes.

"I'm mad about it and embarrassed." I say.

"Me too."

"So, I don't' know how, yet, but I think we have to get over ourselves, and move on." I sigh. This is such a weird conversation. "It's not like you or me to stay down."

"I'm swimming in crap right now, Joel. I won't be moving on any time soon."

"Are you going to see a counselor?" *Please say yes.* I can't be her therapist. I'm so very underqualified for home foreclosures, kids caught in the middle, and broken hearts.

Meryll looks at me like I am nuts. Oops. "Uh, not a marriage counselor, a counselor just for you. You know, to help you move on. That's what we're talking about."

She nods. "Actually, I have my first appointment tonight." She sighs. "Great, now I've got agile coaching and swimming in crap counseling."

Whew.

"Hey, at least you're doing something about it. If you go to counseling tonight, well, *when* you go to counseling tonight, that will be the start of you moving on. To better things and happier things. Right now it's hard to believe you will be in a better place, but you will. You are too smart and strong to stay down."

"I just don't know how I can be bold at work right now. It seems so risky."

"You know, I saw that spark in your eye just a minute ago. When you said your coach was changing things." I smiled. "You know you are meant for bigger things. Whether it's working here or somewhere else, you deserve it. Eve helped me see that in myself. I was struggling so much with what I was starting to see"

She nods. "It's so frickin' scary, Joel. I've got legal and moving bills, and I'm now the sole provider for my kids. If I get fired—"

"That fact that it's now a single income show is all the more reason to use agile coaching to keep changing. You are strengthening yourself and your career. And WL is paying for it. If you stay asleep, you won't be your best. And if you're not your best, your kids won't have your best, either."

"You have no idea what's it's like to lose everything." She starts crying again. "It's so embarrassing. How could I not see the warning signs? How could I have been so blind to all of it? I thought he was getting help…"

"Meryll, I don't know what it's like to feel so devastated or so embarrassed. Or how to be a parent through it all. But running scared is not you. Learning, being curious, and going for it is the Meryll I know and love to work with. You're a great Mom, and you're going to be a great agile leader." Maybe that was too much. I'm in the moment, here, and just want to build up my friend as best I can. Eve would want me to do my best.

"I just…I had no idea that this agile coaching would affect me like this. I'm sure I would have gotten a divorce anyway, but something about this coaching just really threw it in my face. I thought agile coaching would be understanding how to use some new methods to deliver software and get customer feedback. Really, it's all about how I think and how I see things. Or, in my case, how I wasn't seeing things." She leans back in her chair, closes her eyes, and sighs. "Life was simpler without Melvin Milktoast. And unconsciously dreary."

I lean back and close my eyes too. "I also thought it was going to be about tools and customer focus. Every time Eve and I meet, I ask her when we are going to learn about agile. She tells me we are learning about agile. I didn't believe her at first," I laugh. "But the work we've done together has created this huge disturbance in me. I can't tell you how crazy it feels to realize how unhappy I have been at work. Like you said. Life was simpler, and unconsciously dreary."

We're quiet for several minutes, spare Meryll's sniffles. Lost in our thoughts of anger, dismay, and embarrassment. It's a weird new world. Yet it feels safer with two of us feeling this way.

I don't want to push Meryll over the edge, but I feel like this might be the single best opportunity to get her to join me in changing the way she leads. I think she's there, but her confidence is so shaken she can't grab onto it.

"Meryll, I'm your friend first. I am here for you and support you. Jack is too, when you are ready to let him in. He really wants to be a part of our team—"

"Please just tell him for me. If I tell him, I'll have another meltdown. I can't be falling apart like this."

"Fine, but please know that Jack and I are real. Our friendship means something. We will always be here for you, and we will always tell you the truth."

Meryll smiles and wipes away more tears. "Thank you, Joel. Thank you for reminding me of our friendship. I'm sure some of my other friends will pick sides when they find out I dumped Al. I'll probably be left in the dust. But it's comforting to know you and Jack are in my corner." She puts her head in her hands again. "God, I can't even think about how to face my friends."

"The good ones will be there for you, Meryll. You don't have to worry about 'facing them.' They will be there with their arms out, ready to catch you." I smile.

"Thanks for being a great friend, Jack." She looks up and gives me a weak smile back.

"Always."

Meryll sighs. "What you said about being freaked out here at work. I guess I can hold on, as long as you and Jack are in it with me. We're probably in for a wild ride."

"Yes," I laugh. "It already is. And we're only getting started. Just when I think I've got a decent grip on my reality, I'm pointed in yet another direction. It's nuts."

"That's what I'm talking about!"

I assure Meryll she is making the right decision, no matter what else happens. If we stick together, it might be a little less scary, and then we'll grow stronger. Just like when we sat here today, it felt a little safer than being alone. It's apparent now that we've been on a team together, but we have been very alone.

Reflections

Agile coaching is nuts.

Even though I've been on a team, I have been working solo.

Unconsciously dreary vs. freaked out and alive; I'll take freaked out any day.

Francie Van Wirkus

Let's be Frank

"I fired Frank," Jack announces.

"Who?" I can't keep all of his managers straight.

"My coach, Joel."

"Ohhh." I apologize for forgetting about him.

Jack tells me that ending his agreement with Frank was way easier than he thought. He called Frank and told him that he didn't think they were clicking well, and that he wanted a new coach. Sounds simple enough.

But Frank didn't want to let him off the hook without more explanation, so Jack handed it to him. Jack said he wanted more substance, more contact, and less book reading. He could read books on his own, and in fact was doing that before the coaching assignment began. Frank wanted Jack to give it more time, but Jack insisted. So Frank released him, and gave Jack instructions on how to contact the main office and request a new coach.

"What if I get Eve? That would be so dope!" Jack grins.

"That doesn't deserve a response."

"It would be worth it just to see the look on Meryll's face," He chuckles. "Where is she anyway?"

"Attorney appointment. She'll be in later."

"Oh." We both have a moment of guilt. She's going through so much garbage, and our biggest problem is wiggling out from Lora's steely grip.

I break the silence by reminding Jack to ease up on her. He knows, and promises me he will be good. I can't help but remind him. I feel very protective of her after she told me everything she has on her plate right now.

"We should celebrate, Joel. Today was a milestone in our growth." Jack says.

"I don't get it."

"It's the first time in my short career at WL that I kept the power, instead of giving it away to Lora. I didn't need her permission or approval to change agile coaches."

"Most excellent!"

We high five.

"Oh yeah. And I came up with that when I had the crummy coach." Jack's words are full of swagger. "Wait and see what happens when I have a good agile coach."

"Whatever."

Jack and I make a plan to share his victory with Meryll later today. She really needs to see that this victory was as much for Jack as for her or me. We are a real team making real change happen. It's yet another awakening and we want to share it.

Reflections

I am no longer alone at work.

I'm still waking up.

The Discomfort of Breaking Through

I'm back at J&L's café where the manager and team now know me well. It's a good feeling, I guess. It's a cold morning, so the warmth of the café feels more indulgent than ever. Eve and I are doing what we always do: talking about my breakthrough project, reviewing my reflections and past events. Despite the drama of the last few days, I'm feeling upbeat and positive about the changes I made this week. I can see how I'm slowly building one concept on top of another.

Then there is the whole looking for waste experience. My story about finding waste in my swim locker and my garage makes Eve laugh. "Just wait until you go to a grocery store or the airport!"

"Yeah. I can imagine. My wife Cele has always been good about organizing cabinets and closets, and I've been lagging behind. I'm realizing my sloppy ways have probably driven her nuts."

"She'd probably love the concept if you share it in a way that isn't telling her how to do it."

"She did ask about the garden shelving unit…"

"Yep. Best to share it with her so you don't open up a war front at your house."

"Can that be my breakthrough?"

Eve shakes her head no. "Way too easy."

I shrug. It was worth a try.

"What else is on your mind?"

I tell Eve how I've brought Vijay into the fold of *go & see*. He's always been more innovative, reading books, attending conferences, and trying to start study groups. He has a small group of followers, but most of his learning breakthroughs fly under the WL radar. In fact, Vijay is so willing to change the way he works, I find myself looking forward to time with him. No doubt, we've spent more time together the last few weeks than we have the entire time he's worked at WL. Real quality time and also a few laughs. I'm trying to be realistic about my limited knowledge and practice. So I've tried to give him the disclaimer that I don't have a lot of practice, but I'm pretty solid on *go & see*. He assures me that he is a smart guy, and this is enough for him to run with. He is happy to be along for the ride.

It feels so good to have a stronger connection to the work Vijay's team is doing. Using the three questions, there is no awkwardness or confusion about seeing what they are doing. Plus, I'm growing a great relationship with Vijay and the team. If there is no other clarity than these two results, it's still a huge victory.

Sometime soon, I should share our work with other managers, and tell them I'll be working with them soon. I don't want to leave anyone out, but I've got to do this at my own pace. Eve reminds me that my first purpose was to *go & see* with my teams, not to train managers. That will come with time, just like it seemed to naturally happen with Vijay. Right, strengthen *go & see* first, then bring in my managers. At least that strategy feels like the right one for now.

"Have you talked with Vijay about the roadblocks you've experienced with your leadership team, or are you going to let him discover it?"

"I didn't tell him all the stuff I've been telling you, but yeah, I gave him some warning. I want him to know how hard this is, even when it feels like he and the team are doing great things."

"Have you considered that *you* might be one of those roadblocks?"

Well, no. "Uh, I thought when I told him I didn't know what I was doing, that I probably covered that."

Eve offers that now is a great time to pave the way for open dialogue with Vijay in the future. She tells me that as good as I am doing with coaching, it's very likely I'm unknowingly or unconsciously doing things that hold Vijay back from being his best. I sigh. Right. I think I'm a good leader, but really I stink. We have only scratched the surface of what I can do to be my best.

"Maybe that can be my breakthrough, to talk with Vijay?"

Eve is not impressed, giving me her best McKayla Maroney look. Fine, I'll do two assignments that are not my breakthrough, and whatever breakthrough we find that is acceptable. I'm starting to wonder what she has planned for me.

"How are you feeling about Lora and WL today?" Eve sips her matcha. She takes an extra moment to appreciate her drink with a smile.

I nod toward her cup. "They made it just right today?"

"Yes," She sighs. "If only leadership was as easy as dialing in the right amount of honey."

"Right." I admire my own cup of house blend. Who needs honey and fancy Japanese tea when you can have a hot cup of J&L's House Blend? "I'm feeling…stable."

"So, still miserable?"

"Pretty much. I hate how asleep I've been, and I believe I'm still not completely awake. And I hate how I've just let Lora and Rick roll over me for so many years. It's embarrassing."

"Frustrating and embarrassing, but not hopeless."

"No, not hopeless. I'm starting to make small progress strengthening myself, thanks to you and Jack. And, I guess, my own reflection. I can't see myself working somewhere else, but I can at least see it's possible."

Eve nods. "And that, is hope. I like it, Joel." She holds up her hand and we high five. "It's going to be touch and go, up and down, so just hang on to your hope. You're going to do some awesome growing with it."

"It's interesting how our coaching doesn't assume loyalty to the company that is paying for it."

Eve agrees, and assures me that her agile coaching program assumes nothing. Got it.

"How are things with Jack and Meryll? Have you made any progress in building each other up?"

I anticipated talking about that today, but not in a good way. I haven't worked through it all myself, and now there is this mess with Meryll. It's a real sticky spot.

"We had a good discussion together, but then it turned south. Meryll's going through a huge personal problem." I pause, careful not to tell Eve everything.

"I'm sorry to hear that."

"So was I," I sighed. I tell Eve about our intense discussion about our careers at WL, and working for Lora. "You know, this coaching is something else. Meryll said that she didn't see everything that was going on in her personal life until she started agile coaching. She doesn't blame it, but she is really working through some big things as result of it."

Eve smiles. "I've learned over the years, Joel, that agile mindset coaching often crosses over into life coaching, but life coaching rarely crosses over to agile mindset coaching.

"Mindset coaching. That's new."

"Nah. We've been doing it, I'm just calling it out to make a point. Was I successful?"

"Yes."

"You IT people can get so hung up on every word," She sighs.

"That's because I *hang* on your every word, Eve. I'm the newbie."

"Yes, I know you're the newbie," She laughs. "Tell me more."

Wow. For a moment, Jack is in my head, telling me I scored because I have The Hottie. No, don't go there. I have so much respect for Eve, I'm not going to let Jack's damn 16-year old comments ruin this experience.

"It's a summary of all the reflections in my notebook. None of us expected to have our eyes opened the way we have. None of us knew we were asleep at work or at home like we were and are. None of us knew how much power we gave to Lora and Rick."

"How did that conversation go with Jack and Meryll?"

It was one of the most intense and powerful conversations the three of us have ever had. Once again, thank you, agile coaching. I tell Eve that Jack is ready and willing to grow and leave the company, if that's what it takes. His short tenure here is helping him and us. Without him, we would be way behind on this journey.

Meryll is very worried about her personal situation. She is fearful to be bold at work because she really needs her job. Jack and I assured her that we all need our jobs, but more importantly, we talked about how we want to be better leaders, no matter where we work. Right now, we have this new opportunity through coaching that may not last long. It's our chance to go for it and learn how to be the best we can be right now.

"How did you leave it with Meryll?"

"In a good place, I think. I really pushed her to consider how now more than ever, she needs to be her best. I think this connected with her, and so she agreed to join us."

"Sounds like a good start."

"Yes. It was a really difficult conversation, but I'm glad we had it. It's the stuff that makes us stronger in the long run."

"Poor thing. She is lucky to have you and Jack."

"I guess. I mean, the part about being lucky to have us." The silence is full of my worry for Meryll. I keep rewinding my last conversations with Al, when we were on their boat last summer. I'm so blind to everything else, I'm sure I missed something. It really doesn't matter now. Being a good friend and a good teammate is what matters. I hope Jack and I don't let her down.

"What else?" Eve asks.

"I'm not sure if it's okay to tell you this, but Jack fired his coach."

"Tell me more."

"It's kind of a cool story of how we helped each other get to a new place." I share with Eve how Jack noticed he wasn't getting the same caliber of coaching as Meryll and I were. In fact, what he was getting wasn't even coaching. It was more like an online agile literature class. Read books. Talk about the chapter. Read some more. All this meant was that he was falling behind what Meryll and I were learning and practicing.

Now Eve is really interested. "Who was his coach?"

"Frank."

"Oh." There is a flash of recognition on her face, and then it's quickly hidden. "Then what?"

I tell her the great part about Jack realizing he doesn't need to ask Lora permission to switch coaches, and how weird it was for all three of us to grab onto that concept.

"Well done." She smiles. I thought she'd ask me who his new coach was, but she avoided that. She can probably find out what's going on through her network.

She tells me she's impressed with our expectation of good coaching, especially since the coaching was forced on us. We talked about how agile coaching needs good chemistry between the coach and client. With so many mindset discussions, in depth conversations, there can't be room for awkwardness. You don't have to convince me of that. I was asked to stand in a chalk circle inside a busy café. There is no way I would have been conned into doing that by just anyone.

"I like this breakthrough Joel. First, because you did it on your own. You're starting to take some of the constructs we've made, and use them at WL. Even better, you're using them with your team."

"It wasn't all me."

"No, Jack had the idea that he could do it on his own, but Meryll was freaking out about it and you encouraged them both. These little victories add up to huge change over time."

"Thanks."

"Getting Lora, and Rick for that matter, out of your heads is going to take hundreds of victories like this. She's been parked there for a long time, and won't go easily."

"That's the truth." I get mad just thinking about it.

"I believe the three of you are off to a healthy start," She smiles. "It's really important to call out that this coaching is all about you, all for you, Joel. We will always focus first on you. But I hope you see how we can't ignore the connectivity, here. One person's victory on this little team of three is a victory for all of you. Same for the learning moments. I'm sure there will be times when you'll feel like you're learning something they're missing, or the other way around. Remember that none of this change is linear."

"Learning moments," I mock her. "Why not say failure? That if one of us fails, the other two can be impacted by it."

"I could say failure. But what is failure, Joel?"

"Is this my breakthrough project? Another question assignment?" I smile. Those have been really hard.

"No," Eve says flatly. "Stop worrying about your assignment, Joel. I need you to be fully present in what we're talking about right now, instead of worrying about what you're going to have to do. Action is the smaller part of this coaching experience."

Wait a second. I challenge her on that. What about what I do all day long? Isn't that action? No. Eve says most of my job is thinking. So, leader problems are thinking problems. She assures me that you don't learn how to improve your thinking by doing. You improve your thinking by more thinking, and then doing to support that thinking. She makes is sound like it is a natural fact of life. Tell that to someone who has been told to drive for results and deliver more. Action, action, action!

This little part of me begins to feel fearful. Just what is my job if I'm mostly thinking? I don't go there with Eve today. I'm not ready for her to pick apart my brain any more than she is doing at the moment. I'm quiet, hoping she'll forget that I didn't answer her "what is failure?" question.

"So, do you have an answer?"

I guess not.

Eve's got a look like the answer to this question is the most exciting news of the day.

"Failure. It's when something doesn't work right. Something breaks. A bad decision or a wrong decision is made. You forget something, skip over something..." I offer other ideas of mayhem.

"Okay, those are some good corporate calamities. So let's take forgetting something as an example. Let's say you change something on your awesome product, but you forget to tell a work group that it will change how they support the product. What happens next?"

"We'll have a mess of meetings, and we'll have a corrective action plan. We may even form a task force."

"Task force?" Eve squints at me. "Never mind. So these activities are designed to prevent what happened from happening again, right?"

"Sure. And maybe to punish the guilty."

"So, there is learning happening. At least in a healthy business environment, when things go wrong, we take a look at what happened. We try to learn from the experience, right?"

"Right. So we don't make the same mistake again." I nod. "And so the right person can be held accountable."

"Ugh. Joel, I wasn't going to add this concept today, but now we have to. When things go wrong, agile leaders focus on the *process*, not the people. Almost always, business problems are not because of bad people."

"Unless you're cooking the books or reprograming the exhaust on a car."

"Good one!" Eve and I bump fists. "There are always evil people in the world, and so that means they are sometimes the cause of failure. But the key idea in lean and agile is that your people are awesome. Your processes are usually broken."

"Huh."

"I didn't want us to lose that in this discussion. But I really want to hone in on the concept of failure."

"Back to the learning example."

"Yes. Back to the example. Something is forgotten, and there is a flurry of activity to make sure it doesn't happen again, right? You're learning to understand, to correct, to countermeasure, whatever."

"Right."

"So if you learn from this, is forgetting something still a failure?"

"Hmmm."

"What if there was no flurry of activity? What if you did nothing about it? Would that be failure?"

I smile, because I see where she's going with it. "I have an answer. Failure is when you don't try to learn."

"Excellent. So, you don't have to call them learning moments, but they are not failures. When you learn from the experience, even when you learn that you don't have a remedy yet, it is not a failure. I'm not trying to avoid the word, but to put it in its place."

"This is rich," I say. "I will have to think about this for a while."

"Yes you will. *We* will. It's a huge foundational piece for changing the way you think as a leader. And, fair warning now, you will bump into all sorts of madness at WL when you begin practicing this one. Let's leave it there for now; you start thinking about it for yourself and how it fits with your teams. It's a really difficult but fun concept."

"Sounds like you have a lot cooked up for me in the future."

She grins. "Which reminds me. I am taking a vacation starting next week. You get a break from me for two whole weeks."

"Now?" We're just getting started. "You've got to be kidding me."

Eve is way too smug. Pre-vacation smug. "I kid you not. No phone or email access either. So, we're--"

"Do I get a substitute coach?" I know the answer.

"No." Eve wrinkles her nose. "You will be fine. Plus, you'll have a breakthrough project that you'll need two weeks to do."

"Where are you going?" I'm still indignant.

"New Zealand. But this is not about me. It's about setting you up for your next breakthrough project."

"Huh. I suppose you deserve a break," I smirk.

Eve circles back to the first part of our meeting, when we talked about my progress with practicing *go & see.*

"Since you're having such success in this area, I want you to build on it while I'm gone. It will be fun."

"I wasn't worried until you told me it was going to be fun."

"Cancel your one-on-one meetings with Vijay."

"What?"

"You heard me. But only for Vijay."

"You-I can't do that!"

Eve hesitates for a moment, then smiles. "Yes, you can Joel." I can see her struggle to be patient with me.

"How? How would I explain this one away?"

"You're not *explaining it away*. You *go & see* enough, that a one-on-one meeting is waste. Status crap that neither of you need to do, because you are going to Vijay's gemba and the team's gemba."

"Huh." The part of me that is not afraid wants to jump for joy. Maybe this will be fun.

"This is very counter to WL culture, and most others."

I sigh. "You got that right." I sit back to take it all in.

"What do you feel most, Joel, relief or dread?"

"I love it and dread it all at once," I say. "You make it sound simple, but it's not. I don't think it is. This is going to be really hard."

Eve shrugs, "What makes it complicated?"

"Uh. Everything. Every director, manager and team lead has one-on-ones."

"How many of those meetings do you think are waste?"

"Doesn't matter. It's an expectation to have them. How to get past that expectation?"

"So, even if you explained to Vijay the *why behind the what*, he would still want to have one-on-ones?"

"Well no, Vijay wouldn't but—"

Eve tells me that Vijay is the only one who has the right to expect something. Anyone else who believes they have a stake in your one-on-one meetings with Vijay is micro-managing.

"Well, yeah. But isn't that part of what we are trying to change, here? The control?"

"Yes. But I want you to see where the power in this one is. It's with you and Vijay." She pauses for effect. "Not Lora, or Rick or Vijay's team, or anyone else. This assignment is a lot of things: getting rid of waste, trusting the *go & see* philosophy, respecting people, and exploiting command and control behaviors."

"Oh, it's more than that, Eve. What about testing my courage to exploit the command and control behaviors? It's a lot of hard work on my part. You can't just assume that's part of this breakthrough project."

Eve smiles as she crinkles her napkin into a Japanese fan. "You think you need help being courageous?"

"Apparently, I do."

"No. You have plenty of courage, Joel. You just haven't used it in a very long time. Your courage is asleep, and therefore rusty. But it's fully intact. It's my job, and that of the coaching process, to awaken your courage. Once we do that, the rust will fall off, and your courage will once again be fully functional."

I tell Eve I appreciate her confidence, but I'm still feeling very uncomfortable. She asks me if I think it is impossible. No. Well then, she says, she's not worried. Because breakthrough projects are supposed to be very uncomfortable.

"Think it through," She encourages me. She asks me to think of Vijay and how good he will feel knowing he's no longer going to be micromanaged. Think of how his team might respect him and me more because we are being better leaders. With a change for the good in how we lead, we are opening up more growth possibilities for the team and for ourselves.

"Find the words to share with Vijay what you're doing. Find the words to use with Lora and Rick, should they confront you. Or anyone else who might confront you."

I'm there. I'm scared but I'm really psyched to do this. I have to run it past her again to make sure I really get it. I don't want to mess this one up.

"Eve, let me make sure I understand *the why behind the what* as you put it. Since I *go & see* with Vijay and his team, this is my status. When I ask the three questions you gave me, this is how I find out what's going on now, and what problems are out there. When I visit the team and ask the same questions, I'm getting an even deeper understanding of the work. After all that, a one-on-one meeting would be overkill."

"Right. No more status meetings with Vijay. Ever. Special meetings for career development, strategy, or special situations are still needed."

"Got it." I sigh, and my shoulders go down a few inches. "I think I can do it. At least, I'm really excited to try this one."

"I don't have to know Vijay to know that he's going to love it. But he may need your reassurances that you are not dumping him for something or someone else. Be very clear about how practicing *go & see* with him will continue and deepen as you practice more. Offer hope that you two will probably get more out of this than any status meeting you had in the past."

I smile just thinking about the excitement Vijay will have for this change.

"That's the way. You're thinking about Vijay. No more waste." Eve grins and leans back in her chair. "What a great time to take a two week vacation to New Zealand."

"What if I blow it up while you're gone? Is there an agile leader hotline?"

She assures me I will be fine. No hotlines, no last minute changes to the plan. This one is locked and loaded.

I leave J&L's Café with quick steps, really jazzed about what I'm about to do. What a salient moment in my short agile coaching experience. I no longer wonder about how different or how difficult it will be to be an agile leader. It's unlike anything I imagined.

Reflections

Waste is everywhere.

Agile mindset is deep.

Failure is the absence of learning.

My courage is intact.

Control Freak Epidemic

One of my managers, Alexis, invited me back to her team's weekly meeting at 1:00 p.m. This particular team is going to be launching a massive technology upgrade in one of our U.S. sales regions. Alexis thought it would be a good idea for me to attend one, and so I was happy to visit them.

Before I arrive at the conference room, I think about my intent to observe and support. I make sure I'm there on time, but I sit at the back of the table. As Eve would say, *this is not my meeting...*

At 1:00 p.m., the team lead wants to begin the meeting but doesn't. Alexis has not yet arrived, and there are about four other team members missing. We wait. People open their laptops and begin working, checking email. They fully expected not to begin on time. I would have too, if Eve hadn't made me stand in a chalk circle. I resist the temptation to check my phone, and instead make small talk with Aaron, the team member sitting next to me. He's new and we haven't met before, so this delay is working out nicely for us to get acquainted.

At 1:05 p.m., the team lead looks at his watch again, and says we're going to wait one more minute. I'm happily chatting with Aaron, but wonder about Alexis. Looking around the room, no one seems in a hurry. Must be just another team meeting. I know the feeling well.

At 1:08 p.m. we begin the meeting. The team members who are there close their laptops and dig right in. They open up a spreadsheet, projecting it on a screen, and start talking. We are looking at a list of road shows, as the team calls them. Nothing new here. The spreadsheet is used to keep track of where and when people from this team are presenting what they are doing to other teams who will be impacted. Two people are needed to present each road show, so there is healthy exchange about who is going to do what and when. It looks to me like the team is in good shape. In fact, this team has mojo.

One team member, Jim, speaks up that he needs help with a group that he and Aaron have already presented to last week. That group wants them to return for a deeper dive. Apparently, they thought about what they heard and needed more. Jim can't do it because he's going to be on vacation for two weeks. Aaron can do it, but he needs a partner. I can't help but smile. There is a vacation epidemic going around. And, why am I not on vacation?

This is when Alexis walks in and sits down in a seat that the team lead saved for her. It's 1:17 p.m. There is no apology for being late. She checks her phone, and then opens her portfolio to a blank page. It's a lot of things, but it's really distracting.

One team member was asking Jim for more detail about the team before committing to the event.

Alexis interrupts. "This one should be on the spreadsheet with the others. It's really important that all of the road shows are on the list."

The room deflates just a little. Jim clears his throat. "Uh, yeah. We just found out about this one—"

"What do you mean, you just found out about it?" Alexis has no clue what is going on. Should she even be talking right now?

"Uh…" Jim's paralyzed with what to do with her bad behavior.

Alexis jumps in again, "One thing I would advise you to consider with these lists is keeping them as up-to-date as possible so anyone can just pick up the list and go with it."

A few people look at me. I'm focused on Alexis. What is she thinking?

"Alexis, the item we were discussing isn't on the list because it's a different item," Aaron says. Yes, the new guys are brave at WL.

"I don't understand. I—"

"Right." Aaron is a cool cucumber. I was really impressed. "We don't expect you to understand, because we were discussing it before you walked in. There is a team that wants a deeper dive, so we have to circle back with them."

Jim's face is red. It's hard to know if he's embarrassed or angry. If I were him, I might be both.

Alexis shifts uneasily in her seat. "Oh. I see. I just wanted you to make sure you capture all the work you're doing on that list."

"Right. We are doing exactly that, so no worries." Aaron's voice is steady. Jim busies himself writing something in a notebook.

"Great." Alexis' voice is tight as she quickly nods. She's now on the defense.

The meeting picks up again, but this time the mojo is gone. Everyone is feeling the effects of the awkward interruption. They soldier on through the list. Alexis is quiet for the moment.

Later in the discussion, Alexis challenges who is listed as a single point of contact for a work group. "I don't mean to derail your work, here, but have you considered..."

Alexis says this often, but I've never noticed it as a bad thing until now. I always thought she had an honest intent with that statement. After what I experienced earlier in the meeting, it's now very clear she's a control freak. I don't have to know anything about agile or even lean to know that this is just plain old bad leadership. Man, I'm going to have to address this with her.

The team lets her go down the rabbit hole until she is finished. Then they tell her they will carry forward her request. Alexis is pleased. Some team members are looking at me again. I'm starting to feel really uncomfortable. In my new very-awake state, something smells bad about that interaction, too. It's in that control freak category, but with a different twist. I'm not sure what to do with this part, but I'm sure enough about the other sins to give her feedback.

After the meeting, I catch Alexis and ask her if she has five minutes for some feedback. We find an empty conference room, and she immediately apologizes for her team being so disorganized and disconnected to *"what's really happening."*

I assure her that I saw a team with great mojo until she walked into the room late and interrupted them. I give her more details on what the room looked like and felt like. Then the words just came out, as if I had always said them: when you arrive late for a meeting, do not speak for at least as long as you were late. Unless of course you are called upon by someone in the room.

Alexis looks at me like I have two heads. "It's really hard for me to get to this meeting on time because I'm always having a business lunch. And, I said the things I did because they are not interacting with the same people I am. They don't know what I know."

"Your team knows plenty. It's why you hired them." I smile and try to be reassuring, not scolding. "Alexis, just think about what I've said." She tells me she will, and we part ways.

Walking to visit another team, I'm still haunted by the events in that meeting. The most disturbing part of the experience was how the team just rolled over and let her railroad whatever she wanted. Aaron was a cool cucumber because he has experienced the situation many times before and knew just what to say to pacify her. The new guy has more balls, so he's the one who steps forward. He hasn't been beaten down yet. The team is happy to let him push Alexis. *Maybe this time it will work, even though it hasn't ever worked.* The others silently take it, cope with it, do anything but pushback. Oops, there's that word.

This team, they are like me. Giving Alexis all the power. It's an infection in our organization. I want to vomit.

Reflections

Command and control leadership is a rampant epidemic at WL.

I helped spread the epidemic.

I am literally sad about work.

Will agile coaching be enough?

R.I.P. 1X1

The next morning, I meet with Vijay to talk about canceling our one-on-one meetings. I was going to do it yesterday afternoon, but after the meeting with Alexis, I didn't have the energy for my breakthrough project. After a hard bike session last night, and a mind-clearing swim early this morning, I was ready to roll. So, Alexis' behavior in that meeting caused my productivity to tank. That is waste. Wasted time and wasted energy. If Vijay had to move something on his calendar to accommodate my switch, there is more waste. I'm not sure what that is, but Outlook waste has to be one of the most painful kinds of waste, ever.

Vijay is thrilled. He seems to be completely on board and ready to try it. Once again he is anxious to try this concept with his team. He's been practicing *go & see*, and feels ready. I don't think it's a good idea to pile another thing on top of what he's currently learning.

So I didn't tell him no, but I suggested that we get used to it first. Second best, he said, would be for us to share with his team what we are doing. He believes it would be great to show them how we are changing the way we lead. It would also pave the way for Vijay to do more with his team in the future. A fantastic idea. In fact, the whole conversation was easy, and even energizing. It seemed so natural. But then, I wasn't fearful of this part of the change. It's the rest of WL, outside this safe zone, that will give us trouble.

It concerns me enough that Vijay and I talk about it. He agrees that others will question our strategy, so it's good for us to be unified in what we say about what we are doing. Well, there. One small step for me and Vijay, one giant step toward stopping the Control Freak Epidemic.

Reflections

It's not hopeless.

Starting small feels powerful.

Vijay has been waiting for change.

Francie Van Wirkus

Wingman

I'm about to visit Cindy, a manager in my division, when Lora stops me in the hall. Damn.

"Joel! Just who I want to see." Lora gushes. She is exceptionally manic this morning. Maybe it's the powerful look she has in her crisp pinstripes. Probably an $800 designer suit, but what do I care? I'm comfortable in my black, collarless dress shirt from Ralph Lauren.

I greet her, and ask her pleasant questions.

"I want to join you today. Let's do this visit thing you do together," She grins like it's the most brilliant idea ever. "Let's gemba!" She swivels her hips and waits for me to be impressed.

God. For starters, the gemba is a noun not a verb!

"I can be your wingman."

I smile. Right, wingman. More like gemba crasher. Man, I can't say no! I *want* to say no. "Uh, sure. You can join me—"

"Oh great. I knew you'd say yes. And—"

"You can join me under one condition." I put up a hand. Here it goes. "You can only observe. You absolutely must not speak."

She nods. She has no idea. "Right. Yes, I will just be observing in the background."

"No talking." I am nearly condescending.

"Nope. No talking, Joel. Okay, let's go."

I'm waiting for her to lock arms with me and begin singing "We're off to see The Wizard…"

Cindy has a look of muted fear when we arrive at her desk. I try to make her more comfortable by saying that Lora just ran into me in the hall and wanted to join me. That only made it worse. I get that now. Lora's always inserting herself into things. Uninvited, and unwanted.

We push ahead; I ask Cindy questions about what she's doing this week. She tells us about a budget constraint she's having with training two of her "resources." There is an unexpected business need that cropped up, requiring more dev expertise than the team currently has. Her training budget was small this year, and they are in a jam.

Now that I've asked her what she's trying to do, I ask her what she's tried so far. That's when Lora jumps in.

"I'm sorry. I know I'm just supposed to be observing, but I simply have to ask," Lora smiles. "Have you tried talking with Chase's team? He might have someone with this expertise. I say that because…" Lora rattles on about what she thinks she knows about unique dev skills, which is nothing.

Reluctantly, Cindy agreed to talk with Chase. Of course she did. We are all sick with the Control Freak Epidemic. I try to pull us back on track, asking again, what else she has tried. Lora interjects again, "Can I offer some context here?"

We've now moved past overreaching the role of observing to full-on command and control. Of course she can offer context and tell Cindy what to do. Cindy graciously gives her the floor. For all she knows, this is the way *go & see* is supposed to work.

Lora gives us a big explanation about budgeting, our strategy for the year, and even wanders off track to talk about how we are "rolling out" agile later this year. My head spins as my *go & see* is now *Go off the Rails*. What must Cindy be thinking right now? Did I just hear three different phones vibrate?

How can I stop her? I can't just tell her to shut up. Not with good results anyway. Maybe I can't stop her, but can I salvage this time with Cindy. I need…Eve. Actually, I need…courage. Where is my courage?

"Lora, how about you let Cindy and I talk it through?"

"I'm sorry." She looks sincere. I definitely hear phones vibrating. "I didn't want to derail your work here, but I saw a connection that I wanted to make sure Cindy knew about. I promise I'll be quiet from herein." She tries to look cute. Tries.

Cindy and I talk for another five minutes, but the moment is lost and going south fast. Lora's control freak interruptions were one thing, but now we're on to awkwardness as Lora struggles to keep her mouth shut. She's practically popping the pinstripes off her suit trying to keep quiet. In the end, she can't do it.

"One thing I would advise you to do is to bring your team lead along with this."

"Right." Cindy pacifies her. "We're on it."

"Great to hear." Lora really is having the time of her life. "Let me know if you need more background, or if you need me to help get Chase involved." More display of power, not that I care at this point.

Cindy and I agree to wrap it up, and talk again soon. Neither of us offer that I'm scheduled to come back and visit tomorrow.

Lora talks at me all the way back to my office. I use the time to plan how to give her feedback about demolishing my time with Cindy. I did the thinking; time for action, not for rolling over and playing dead.

"So Joel, when can we do that again?" Lora smooths her lapel. She really likes herself in that suit. "I want to learn more about what you're doing so I can do it too. It looks like something I should be doing."

"Not for a while. I--"

"What do you mean, not for a while?"

"Lora, I don't think it's a good idea for you to join me right now. I need practice, and my managers need practice. When you come along, you can't just observe. You end up taking over the conversation, then neither the manager nor I get our practice."

"But, Cindy needed to know that Chase might be able to help." Lora's voice is getting tight. Ugh.

"That is not the point, Lora. Cindy and I need time to work together without interruption. I know you want to observe quietly, but the truth is, you can't. You derailed our meeting today."

"Yes, and a good thing, too." Lora knows everything. "Cindy had no idea what to do next. If I hadn't been there to tell her--"

I put my hand up. "Lora, you derailed my meeting with Cindy. That can't happen anymore. You can't tag along with me."

"Fine." Lora's nose twitches and her shoulders stiffen. "No more tagging along."

She says a quick good bye and she's gone. I go in my office, close the door, and lean against it in relief. For the second time in two days, I think I'm going to be ill. Such is the tradeoff of being awake and realizing all the crap that is happening around you. And everyone else.

Not long ago I was woefully unconscious, but rather comfortable. Now, I'm working myself to being fully alert, and it's the most uncomfortable journey ever.

Reflections

My courage is intact!

Lora probably doesn't know what to do with my courage. This is scary.

I'm still not awake enough to be a good leader.

I'm still very uncomfortable.

I feel uneasy without a coaching meeting for two whole weeks.

We are going Agile

Jack, Meryll, and I huddle in my office an hour before a big division conference call. We usually have these meetings in person, but this one is an exception because Lora and Rick are traveling.

Jack notes it's poor form to host a division meeting over the phone. Meryll doesn't think it's that big of a deal, but I agree with Jack.

"I learned from my coach that leaders should always choose in-person meetings first."

"Well how practical is that when they are in Miami?" Meryll asks but doesn't really want an answer.

"Hey, you got your new coach!"

"Yup. His name is Steve, and after just one meeting, he's awesome."

"So, is he a hottie?" I ask, just to press Meryll's buttons.

"No." Jack feigns extreme disappointment.

Meryll rolls her eyes, but she has a faint smile. "God, you two never stop."

"It's very disappointing but," Jack holds up his index finger, "what he lacks in hotness, he makes up for in coaching. At least, I think he does."

"How can you know that already?" Meryll is suspicious. I notice she is looking about 25% less haggard than last week.

"Because he met with me in person, and didn't assign any books for me to read. So right there, he's light years ahead of Frank. In fact, we talked about the concept of being present where the work is. If they can't do it from Miami, maybe their timing is off."

"Lora usually has bad timing," Meryll quips.

"You just made a joke." I smile at Meryll. "And you look much better than the last time I saw you."

"Yeah, you're lookin' good, Meryll." Jack playfully punches her arm. "It's nice to see you smile."

She thanks us and announces that her therapist suggested she get a dog. Now her face really lights up. Later today, she and the kids are going to pick up a young rescue dog. He's a Labrador mix, perfect for her kids and for Meryll to run with.

"Sounds great, Meryll. I remember when you used to run. You loved it," I say.

"Yeah," she looks wistful, "I sort of got away from that after kid three. It's time I start taking back my life. It's going to feel so damn good."

Jack and I give her high fives and she soaks it in. Then her face turns serious. "So, anyone know what this meeting is going to cover? It's 90 minutes long."

"It's probably about agile," I say. "I don't know for sure."

Jack agrees. He said he's heard rumblings that Lora and Rick want to get rolling on starting agile at WL. Plus, agile is the topic of the next director team summit. He also heard that they are going to start with a few teams from Ben's area. Ben is a director, but he reports to Rick the CIO. He has a bunch of app dev managers under him. If you're not familiar with IT, this means Ben leads the people who actually make the software. Seems like a logical place to begin agile, since agile was originally about making better software. From the little bit I know of agile, anyway. I can't help but wonder when my teams will get agile.

In his middle forties, Ben is laid back compared to his other director peers. He's been at WL for about three years, so he's still a baby in WL terms of service. I like him, and so do Jack and Meryll. His managers, however, are another story. They are running around like chickens. I'm not sure if the pressure is from Ben or self-imposed, but his area has a reputation for being high strung. They have one crisis after another. Outages, technical debt, you name it. My world has its own set of problems, but Ben's are noisy, rattling around our entire organization.

"This is why we are better together. Between the three of us, someone knows what's going on. Since we don't get much vision, we have to cobble it together. We're so much stronger this way," I say.

"Well, it's just gossip. But in my short time here, I've learned that all WL gossip has some truth to it. And, yeah, I've learned that the vision isn't shared much."

The conference call is about to begin, so I get my PC set up so all of us can see and hear the presentation.

"All we need is popcorn," Meryll mumbles.

Jack laughs. "Good luck having an appetite after Lora talks. Best diet ever."

Rick kicks off the meeting with the usual thank yous. He apologizes for not hosting the meeting in person, but they felt a strong need to communicate what's happening at WL today. Rick is pleased to announce that we will be "rolling out" agile at WL. We will begin with the tech division, specifically the application development areas.

Rick acknowledges the amount of change happening all around us. Now more than ever, we need to be more flexible and responsive to what our sales force needs, and ultimately, what our customers need. Unfortunately, WL's software development is not able to keep up. Which means that our project portfolios can't keep up with changing business priorities. We need to raise our game, be a more engaged partner, and offer the right product at the right time. The time is now for WL to go agile and change our trajectory. Agile will not be easy, and it is not designed to save money. Rick assures us it's a "paradigm shift" to think differently, but he's confident we are up for the challenge.

"My colleague Lora has more details for you." Rick quickly passes control to Lora. *Colleague*? Really?

Lora immediately gets into the weeds of how Ben's area of app dev will be the first focus. They've selected a local agile training firm, and four teams and their managers will go to Scrum training. We don't know what it all means, but we have some very brave teams and managers willing to give it a try. There will also be some supporting resources and leaders attending this training. She can't tell us enough how very pleased she is that people are willing to take a risk to help make WL better. She makes is sound like they are going to jump off a cliff. I guess in her mind, they are.

Although there are just four teams "going Scrum," our entire organization will be impacted. This change will be a disruption, at best. We'll have challenging days and victories, and we'll "have to meet people where they are" in order to make it through. We'll have to work together to "commonize" what we learn about agile, and share it with the organization. In fact, our customers may or may not want agile, but we have to change. We have to listen to their needs, but we have to change. We are in the midst of a catchfall, and need to support each other.

Jack silently mouths the word "catchfall" at me and Meryll with a questioning look. We both shrug. I was still hung up on *commonize*. Not to be confused with communize. Where on earth do they get these words?

During the Q & A section, someone asks what the vision is from the executives, other than we are going agile. Rick takes the question and says that it's not all worked out yet, but we are going to take a bottom up implementation of agile with top down support. We want the growth to happen organically.

The three of us look at each other after that comment. Meryll just shakes her head no and sighs. Not no to growing organically, but no way is that going to happen here. How could it?

Rick continues. "It's very likely that our executives will form some vision around agile in the very near future. But they didn't want to get in the way of getting started."

Meryll wrinkles her nose and whispers, "Very likely? Didn't want to get in the way?"

The call is silent. "Anyone else br-rave enough to ask a question?" Rick smiles. It's almost like taunting. *Anyone willing to step up to the line and take a punch?* Hell no. More crickets. We all know better.

Finally, another question about the executive level vision. Did they offer something they want measured? Any thoughts on metrics? Lora takes the question stating that initially, we are going to measure success with the help of the firm who is training our teams. And, we'll measure the number of scrum teams we have. Our goal for this first year is to have 25% of potential teams going Scrum.

Jack raises his eyebrows. I wonder what Eve would think of all this. Man, it's another week before she returns from New Zealand.

Now the vanity questions roll in. The ones we've been socially engineered to ask here at WL. Gotta look like you are fully engaged in the meeting. Have to show that you are thinking ahead, even when it's completely ambiguous what's ahead. What will this look like? What will it look like for other teams? What will it look like for our impacted business partners? What will it look like for leaders? Speculate, speculate!

Another pie in the sky question pops up: "What do you feel is our greatest challenge with going agile?"

Lora answers that the most difficult challenge will be mobilizing the training for all of our teams and impacted partners. The training lasts for five full days. There is a two-day class for those on the peripheral of a Scrum team. Both are immersive sessions. We see the hardship in this type of commitment, so we are investigating ways to make it shorter than five days. We know the time commitment is a big problem.

Commitment for things of importance in general is a big problem. We can't get people to show up to meetings on time; how would they ever see the value in a five-day class? Not once did she mention that some of our leaders are getting agile coaching. Why was that left out? I hope it doesn't mean we're going to discontinue it. I've already decided if Lora ever pulls the plug on coaching, I'm going to keep going on my own.

Speaking of going solo, someone in the meeting asks if they have to wait to get training. Can they just go get some on their own? Even if it's not the five day kind? Lora shut that down immediately, stating that they do not have the training strategy figured out yet. Let's get these four teams stood up first, and then go from there.

Then comes the question that sends all three of us into silent fits of laughter: "Who will pay for the training?"

Lora starts offering some context, and then Rick jumps in to rescue her from the weeds. "We don't need to get into that here. Please understand agile is a priority."

There were no more questions, so the meeting closed. But don't be fooled. There most certainly will be the meeting after the meeting all around WL tech areas. Lora gives us a link to the PowerPoint presentation she and Rick used, and advises us to share it with our teams. She and Rick are always available for questions, see you at the director team summit, yadda yadda, and the meeting ends.

The three of us stare at each other. We're not stunned because we knew this was coming. We are struggling to sort through all of the different messages within the call.

"What the hell does *'commonize'* mean?" Meryll laughs.

"Well," Jack has a hand to his chin, "it's a paradigm shift on many levels. We are in a catchfall, so it will be challenging."

Meryll's having fun. "Our focus is here, no, wait! I mean, our focus is over *here.*"

It's late, so we break and go our separate ways. I have a hockey tournament to watch.

Driving to the ice rink, I'm rewinding the messages from the division meeting. If I'm going to put together a message for my managers, I sure as hell want it to be less confusing than what I just experienced.

Out of all the mixed messages and corporate speak, one message keeps bothering me. It's Lora's answer on what she thinks is WL's greatest challenge with going agile. She said it was mobilizing training for everyone who needs it.

I don't know much about agile, but from what I do know, Lora's answer is wrong. Our greatest challenge with going agile is…us.

To be continued...

Join Joel as he continues his journey—often times a slog—to become an agile leader. In book two, Joel is once again pushed to his limits by Eve and by his own vision to become a great agile leader. He'll learn the agile manifesto and all five elements of lean leadership. This will come in handy as his team collides with Ben's newly agile dev teams. Joel also begins working with his Ironman coach. It's a lot to take on; is it too much?

Meanwhile, Meryll slowly pulls out of her divorce, and begins strengthening herself as a leader and a Mom. She asks her team for feedback on her leadership, and gets an earful. Jack's new guy status has all but evaporated, so he faces new challenges and pressure to conform. He's finding his three month refreshes coming on faster than he's comfortable. Is he losing his mojo and getting sucked in to WL for good?

The culture at WL is stronger than ever, creating a force of opposition Joel must face with Lora and Rick. Then there is hope…Joel accomplishes just one tiny breakthrough with Rick about his calendar, and it sets off a chain of events, forever changing tech at WL. The Dominant Gene series continues…will your Agile leader journey continue?

Author Biography

A conqueror of mediocrity, Francie Van Wirkus is a Lean Agile coach in the insurance and financial services industry, helping people take sustainable steps toward their goals. Her innovative ways of leading and sustaining change have helped lead a large IT transformation effort. Francie is a certified coach, keynote speaker, author, and host of CL&I Radio, an internal corporate radio show focused on all things continuous learning and improvement.

She is and active Agile and Lean blogger, and co-host of Agile Bettys, a motivational podcast about living an agile lifestyle. Francie enjoys racing in Ironman competitions and lives in Wisconsin with her husband and three delightful children. She is currently working on book two of The Dominant Gene series.

www.francievanwirkus.com

www.agilebettys.com

Email

francievanwirkusinspire@gmail.com

info@agilebettys.com

Francie can also meet you on Linkedin, Twitter, and Instagram.